Pagan Portals
&
Shaman Pathways

...an ever-growing library of shared knowledge.

Moon Books has created two unique series where leading authors and practitioners come together to share their knowledge, passion and expertise across the complete Pagan spectrum. If you would like to contribute to either series, our proposal procedure is simple and quick, just visit our website (www.MoonBooks.net) and click on Author Inquiry to begin the process.

If you are a reader with a comment about a book or a suggestion for a title we'd love to hear from you! You can find us at facebook.com/MoonBooks or you can keep up to date with new releases etc on our dedicated Portals page at facebook.com/paganportalsandshamanpathways/

'Moon Books has achieved that rare feat of being synonymous with top-quality authorship AND being endlessly innovative and exciting.'
Kate Large, Pa

T0159486

Pagan Portals

Animal Magic, Rachel Patterson
An introduction to the world of animal magic and working with animal spirit guides

Australian Druidry, Julie Brett
Connect with the magic of the southern land, its seasons, animals, plants and spirits

Blacksmith Gods, Pete Jennings
Exploring dark folk tales and customs alongside the magic and myths of the blacksmith Gods through time and place

Brigid, Morgan Daimler
Meeting the Celtic Goddess of Poetry, Forge, and Healing Well

By Spellbook & Candle, Mélusine Draco
Why go to the bother of cursing, when a bottling or binding can be just as effective?

By Wolfsbane & Mandrake Root, Mélusine Draco
A study of poisonous plants, many of which have beneficial uses in both domestic medicine and magic

Candle Magic, Lucya Starza
Using candles in simple spells, seasonal rituals and essential craft techniques

Celtic Witchcraft, Mabh Savage
Wield winds of wyrd, dive into pools of wisdom; walk side by side with the Tuatha Dé Danann

Dancing with Nemetona, Joanna van der Hoeven
An in-depth look at a little-known Goddess who can help bring peace and sanctuary into your life

Fairy Witchcraft, Morgan Daimler
A guidebook for those seeking a path that combines modern Neopagan witchcraft with the older Celtic Fairy Faith

God-Speaking, Judith O'Grady
What can we do to save the planet? Three Rs are not enough. Reduce, reuse, recycle...and religion

Gods and Goddesses of Ireland,
Meet the Gods and Goddesses of Pagan Ireland in myth and modern practice

Grimalkyn: The Witch's Cat, Martha Gray
A mystical insight into the cat as a power animal

Hedge Riding, Harmonia Saille
The hedge is the symbolic boundary between the two worlds and this book will teach you how to cross that hedge

Hedge Witchcraft, Harmonia Saille
Learning by experiencing is about trusting your instincts and connecting with your inner spirit

Hekate, Vivienne Moss
The Goddess of Witches, Queen of Shades and Shadows, and the ever-eternal Dark Muse haunts the pages of this poetic devotional, enchanting those who love Her with the charm only this Dark Goddess can bring

Herbs of the Sun, Moon and Planets, Steve Andrews
The planets that rule over herbs that grow on Earth

Hoodoo, Rachel Patterson
Learn about and experience the fascinating magical art of
Hoodoo

Irish Paganism, Morgan Daimler
Reconstructing the beliefs and practices of pre-Christian Irish
Paganism for the modern world

Kitchen Witchcraft, Rachel Patterson
Take a glimpse at the workings of a Kitchen Witch and share in
the crafts

Meditation, Rachel Patterson
An introduction to the beautiful world of meditation

Merlin: Once and Future Wizard, Elen Sentier
Merlin in history, Merlin in mythology, Merlin through the
ages and his continuing relevance

Moon Magic, Rachel Patterson
An introduction to working with the phases of the Moon

Nature Mystics, Rebecca Beattie
Tracing the literary origins of modern Paganism

Pan, Mélusine Draco
An historical, mythological and magical insight into the God Pan

Pathworking through Poetry, Fiona Tinker
Discover the esoteric knowledge in the works of Yeats,
O'Sullivan and other poets

Runes, Kylie Holmes
The Runes are a set of 24 symbols that are steeped in history, myths and legends. This book offers practical and accessible information for anyone to understand this ancient form of divination

Sacred Sex and Magick, Web PATH Center
Wrap up ecstasy in love to create powerful magick, spells and healing

Spirituality without Structure, Nimue Brown
The only meaningful spiritual journey is the one you consciously undertake

The Awen Alone, Joanna van der Hoeven
An introductory guide for the solitary Druid

The Cailleach, Rachel Patterson
Goddess of the ancestors, wisdom that comes with age, the weather, time, shape-shifting and winter

The Morrigan, Morgan Daimler
On shadowed wings and in raven's call, meet the ancient Irish Goddess of war, battle, prophecy, death, sovereignty, and magic

Urban Ovate, Brendan Howlin
Simple, accessible techniques to bring Druidry to the wider public

Your Faery Magic, Halo Quin
Tap into your Natural Magic and become the Fey you are

Zen Druidry, Joanna van der Hoeven

Zen teachings and Druidry combine to create a peaceful life
path that is completely dedicated to the here and now

Shaman Pathways

Aubry's Dog, Melusine Draco

A practical and essential guide to using canine magical energies

Black Horse White Horse, Mélusine Draco

Feel the power and freedom as Black Horse, White Horse
guides you down the magical path of this most noble animal

Celtic Chakras, Elen Sentier

Tread the British native shaman's path, explore the Goddess
hidden in the ancient stories; walk the Celtic chakra spiral
labyrinth

Druid Shaman, Danu Forest

A practical guide to Celtic shamanism with exercises and
techniques as well as traditional lore for exploring the Celtic
Otherworld

Elen of the Ways, Elen Sentier

British shamanism has largely been forgotten: the reindeer
Goddess of the ancient Boreal forest is shrouded in mystery...
follow her deer-trods to rediscover her old ways

Following the Deer Trods, Elen Sentier

A practical handbook for anyone wanting to begin the old
British paths. Follows on from Elen of the Ways

Trees of the Goddess, Elen Sentier
Work with the trees of the Goddess and the old ways of Britain

Way of the Faery Shaman, Flavia Kate Peters
Your practical insight into Faeries and the elements they engage
to unlock real magic that is waiting to help you

Web of Life, Yvonne Ryves
A new approach to using ancient ways in these contemporary
and often challenging times to weave your life path

Pagan Portals
The Power of
the Elements

A Magical Approach to Earth, Air,
Fire, Water & Spirit

Pagan Portals

The Power of the Elements

A Magical Approach to Earth, Air, Fire, Water & Spirit

Mélusine Draco

Winchester, UK
Washington, USA

First published by Moon Books, 2018
Moon Books is an imprint of John Hunt Publishing Ltd., No. 3 East St., Alresford,
Hampshire SO24 9EE, UK
office1@jhpbooks.net
www.johnhuntpublishing.com
www.moon-books.net

For distributor details and how to order please visit the 'Ordering' section on our website.

Text copyright: Mélusine Draco 2017

ISBN: 978 1 78535 916 3
978 1 78535 917 0 (ebook)
Library of Congress Control Number: 2017960098

A CIP catalogue record for this book is available from the British Library.

Design: Stuart Davies

Printed and bound by CPI Group (UK) Ltd, Croydon, CR0 4YY, UK

We operate a distinctive and ethical publishing philosophy in
all areas of our business, from our global network of authors to
production and worldwide distribution.

Contents

For Adrien ... who keeps on asking the questions

In the Beginning ...

A magical practitioner, whether witch, druid, ritual magician or shaman must be aware that there are all manner of different currents and movements on the planet that affect us on a deeper magico-mystical level than we could ever imagine when we begin our voyage of discovery. And as I asked at the beginning of *Traditional Witchcraft and the Path to the Mysteries,* do we ever stop to think that the burst of energy that sets the pendulum swinging could be caused by the swirling molten layer under the Earth's crust, creating the electro-magnetic field that surrounds the planet by the spinning outer crust around the solid part of the inner core? Do we recognise the continuous re-arranging of the Earth's surface by tectonic plate movement; of the earthly debris from volcanoes that brings precious stones and minerals to the surface and the underground eruptions that causes giant *tsunami* to race around the globe. Or is our **Elemental Earth** just a quiet ramble in the countryside and a container of sand marking the Northern quarter in our magic Circle?

We may sit meditating by a rippling stream, watching the sunlight dance in the water as it trips over the stones and pebbles in its path – but do we allow our minds to explore the greater picture of where that crystal clear water comes from? Do we realise that this stream began its brief chapter of life being drawn up as vapour from the ocean and falling as rain on the hills and mountain sides, before flowing down into the river valley with enough power to bring rocks and stones tumbling in its wake? Do our magical energies focus on the stream; the rainfall on the mountain; or the ocean? Are we constantly aware of the force of that water-flow throughout the seasons – the spring floods; the summer drought; the clogging of the channel with autumn leaves and the frozen surface in winter. Or does our concept of **Elemental Water** begin and end with the symbolic bowl of tap water marking the Western quarter in our magic Circle?

Nothing on the planet can live without clean, breathable air, but a magical practitioner needs to think beyond soft summer breezes and rainbows after a spring shower. Air is the stuff from which tornadoes and hurricanes are made; it brings puffs of cumulus clouds or a billowing thunderhead some ten miles high; not to mention the thousands-of-feet-high dust storms that are created when a monsoon collides with dry air currents above it. Or is our **Elemental Air** merely the curling smoke from a perfumed joss stick marking the Eastern quarter in our magical workings?

Fire, even in its most modest form has the capacity for great destruction – a box of matches in the hands of a child, a fallen candle, or a carelessly discarded cigarette. On a grander and more epic scale, we are well acquainted by television coverage with devastating wildfire destroying anything that stands in its path; the eruption of a volcano; or the power of solar winds that reach out from the sun to interfere with electronic equipment here on Earth. Or is our contact with **Elemental Fire** restricted to a candle burning at the Southern quarter of our Circle?

For over two thousand years of human history there were just the classical elements of the ancient Greeks – earth, air, fire and water – who formulated this idea in the sixth century BCE. The Greeks had an insatiable curiosity about the workings of the world and came to the conclusion that there was a logical explanation for natural phenomenon that was *not* caused by dyspeptic deities or any other supplicatory supernatural agencies. These ancient men of science at first believed that a single element was the fundamental principle of the universe but eventually the natural philosopher Empedocles argued that all four played equal and interactive parts.

These essential four, he expounded in *Tetrasomia*, or *Doctrine of the Four Elements*, either singly or in combination, account for all matter on Earth. That 'things take on different forms when their component elements separate and rearrange, variously directed by the force of Love, which brings elements together, and Strife, which tears them apart'. And as Dr Rebecca Rupp pointed out in *Four Elements*: 'The theory revealed a surprising grasp of the basics: that is, all matter is assembled from a finite number of basic and irreducible elements; and these, combined in specific proportions, make up all the substances that exist.'

In reality, none of these, apart from water, was even close to being elemental. As Marcus Chown explained in *The Magic Furnace*, all that was needed was for someone to draw the *right* conclusion.

The man who did so was Antoine Lavoisier, a French aristocrat whose life was ended by the guillotine in the spring of 1794 ... Five years before his death, Lavoisier compiled the first list of substances which he believed could not by any means, be broken down into simpler substances. Lavoisier's list consisted of 23 'elements'. Some later turned out not to be elements at all but many were indeed elemental. They included sulphur and mercury, iron and zinc, silver and gold. Lavoisier's scheme was a turning point in the history of science. It signalled the death of alchemy and the birth of chemistry.

Nevertheless, the contemporary pagan viewpoint is that the four classical elements are still a natural part of our mental make-up, though in each person only one predominates. There is still a lurking appeal of the ancient Greek view that a single one-word answer can reveal something about what we are. In truth, science has come a long way since then ... and so has magic. The Greek four are the elements of tradition and time, and have dominated human thought for over two millennia – and have been around long enough to insinuate themselves into our lives, language, art and literature. Even Galen, the 'Father of Medicine' cited elemental properties as being at the root of sickness; a theory that was still being expounded by the seventeenth-century herbalist,

3

apothecary and astrologer Nicholas Culpeper.

In magical practice, these four elements still guard the four cardinal points of the Compass (or Circle) and it doesn't matter in whose name, or in what form we summon them. When 'Calling the Quarters' for a Magic Circle it is usual to draw down the protection of the elements by summoning the:

Guardian of the Watchtowers of the North, South, East, West ...

Or:

The Power of the Element of Earth, Fire, Air, Water ...

Or:

The Guardian of the North, South, East, West ...

Or:

The Element of Earth, Fire, Air, Water ...

Or:

The Stations of the Gnomes, Salamanders, Sylphs and Undines.

The last comes from the classical Paracelsian perspective that there are four elemental categories: gnomes, undines, sylphs, and salamanders, which correspond to the Classical elements of antiquity: earth, water, air and fire. Aether (quintessence) was not assigned an elemental and represents the realm of spirit. For those of ritual magic persuasion the Call would be for the archangels from the Hebrew tradition:

North = Earth = Uriel
South = Fire = Michael
East = Air = Raphael
West = Water = Gabriel

And there is a very good reason why we do this, as Kenneth Grant explained so well in *Hecate's Fountain*:

It may be asked, why then do we not abandon the ancient symbols in favour of the formulae of nuclear physics and quantum mechanics? The answer is that the occultist understands that contact with these energies may be established more completely through symbols so ancient that they have had time to bury themselves in the vast storehouse of the racial subconsciousness. To such symbols the Forces respond swiftly and with incalculable fullness, whereas the pseudo-symbols manufactured in the laboratory possess no link with elements in the psyche to which they can appeal. The twisting and turning tunnels explored laboriously by science lead, only too often, away from the goal. The intellectual formulæ and symbols of mathematics have been evolved too recently to serve as direct conduits. For the Old Ones, such lines of communication are dead. The magician, therefore, uses the more direct paths which long ages have been mapped out in the shadowlands of the subconsciousness.

And since I go along with Crowley's belief that magic is a blend of science and art, it is easy to see how '*sulphur and mercury, iron and zinc, silver and gold*' later became the magical correspondences for the Underworld, Mercury, Mars, Uranus, Moon and the Sun respectively. It is true Uranus wasn't universally accepted as a new planet until it was 'discovered' by William Herschel in 1783 but it had been observed on many occasions over the centuries and mistaken for a star. Possibly the earliest known observation was by Hipparchus, who in 128 BCE might have recorded it in his star catalogue that was later incorporated into Ptolemy's *Almagest*.

And although zinc was recorded as an 'element' by the unfortunate *Antoine Lavoisier* in 1789, ornaments made of alloys containing 80–90% zinc have been found that are 2500 years old, while a paper published in 1933 (Weeks, *The Discovery of the Elements*), cites a possibly prehistoric statuette containing 87.5% zinc found at a Dacian archaeological site. The smelting of zinc ores with copper was apparently discovered in Cyprus and was used later by the Romans. Alchemists burned zinc metal in air and collected the resulting zinc oxide calling it *Lana philosophica*, Latin for 'philosopher's wool', because it collected in wooly tufts like white snow. The name of the metal was probably first documented by Paracelsus, a Swiss-born German alchemist and magician, who referred to the metal as 'zincum' in his book *Liber Mineralium II*, in the sixteenth century, before the metal was rediscovered later in Europe.

These ancient symbols are magical shorthand that cut across the aeons and connect us with the 'Old Ones' who are quite willing to pick up and communicate with those who 'speak' their language. And to repeat with emphasis what Kenneth Grant wrote on the subject:

> *To such symbols the Forces respond swiftly and with incalculable fullness, whereas the pseudo-symbols manufactured in the laboratory possess no link with elements in the psyche to which they can appeal ... The magician, therefore, uses the more direct paths which long ages have been mapped out in the shadowlands of the subconsciousness.*

Nevertheless, the idea for this book came from a Coven member who was involved in the filming of an opera on a beach at low tide:

> As we were shooting the film, the tide was starting to come in quite quickly and every five minutes we had to move forward because the water was catching up with us. Standing there I could feel the immense power of the energy that was rising right behind me. The wind was picking up and I could sense the power of the water. It was incredible. All I wanted to do was stop shooting this stupid film and work some magic! It also made me think that I wanted to go and live right by the sea so I could experience this more often. It was so amazing. And then it made me think about the conversation we had

the other day when you asked about 'Calling the Quarters' in the Circle. You said you thought I was more connected to Water and I said, *No, Air*. Well boy, did I feel connected to that water. I can feel it now. When I need to call upon Water I will dig inside of me for that feeling I had. I can connect to Air as well but I think you were right, I think I have a much stronger connection to Water for some reason. Perhaps because I miss it, being from Marseille in the south of France, but now that I am on this path I feel like I miss it even more.

Here we have the realisation that although we are psychically connected to the same elements as our ancient Greek counterparts, the modern belief that in 'each of us only one predominates' is a long way from the truth. In ancient astrology, the triple groupings of the 'Star Signs' were more of a seasonal nature, so each season was given the qualities of a particular element. For example:

- Spring (wet becoming hot) – Air – Aries, Taurus, Gemini
- Summer (hot becoming dry) – Fire – Cancer, Leo, Virgo
- Autumn (dry becoming cold) – Earth – Libra, Scorpio, Sagittarius
- Winter (cold becoming wet) – Water – Capricorn, Aquarius, Pisces

All the fire signs are by their nature hot and dry. However, the addition of the elemental qualities of the seasons results in differences between the fire signs; Leo being the midsummer sign gets a double dose of hot and dry and is the pure fire sign. Aries being a spring sign is wetter (hot & dry, hot & wet), and Sagittarius being an autumnal sign is colder (hot & dry, cold & dry); and in the Southern Hemisphere the seasonal cycle is, of course, reversed. Using the seasonal qualities also accounts for other differences in expression between signs of the same element.

Similarly, if we look again at Nicholas Culpeper's *Herbal*, we can see how this seventeenth-century English herbalist's medicine was the same as that practised by the famous Greek physicians Hippocrates and Galen that had been used traditionally throughout Europe for 1,400 years: 'The four temperaments of the body, then, were said to arise from the interaction of the four elements and their primary qualities. This four-fold variation in the human body was matched specifically by the predominance of one of the four humours or bodily fluids. Indeed, the humours, elements, qualities and temperaments were all related', observed Graeme Tobyn in *Culpeper's Medicine* when describing the seventeenth-century's approach to medicine, although the influence of astrology began to wane in the decades following Culpeper's death.

The elements Earth, Air, Fire and Water were not literally viewed as things in this world, but as the building blocks in the composition of everything in Nature. Soil would be said to be formed of all elements but, in this case, with a preponderance of the element Earth so that it was perceived as being earthy. Likewise, Air contained Fire (heat), Water (Vapour) and Earth (particles) as well as, mainly Air. The philosopher Empedocles' (c. 490–430 BCE) ideas became truly established in Greek physics and natural philosophy when the great philosophers Plato and Aristotle incorporated it into their theories concerning the physical universe.

> Empedocles might have watched a piece of wood burning. Something disintegrates. We hear it crackle and splutter. That is *water*. Something goes up in smoke. That is *air*. The *fire* we can see. Something also remains when the fire is extinguished. That is the ashes – or *earth*. (Gaarder, *Sophie's World*)

And to put these ideas into a magical context, we discover

that each element has other facets influencing its purity or effectiveness. By using the Court Cards of our favourite Tarot Deck we can begin to identify what causes those peculiarities that make us say we don't identify with our particular Star Sign. Leo, for example, is represented by **Elemental Fire** and is identified with the Knight (or King) of Wands but his 'family' is made up of the Princess (*the Earthy part of Fire*) and the Prince (*the Airy part of Fire*) of Wands ... and the Queen of Wands (*the Watery part of Fire*).

Adrien, being an Aquarian and a professionally trained singer and dancer, is obviously more geared towards the *Watery Part of Air*, while I'm an untypical Piscean wired for the *Fiery Part of Water* in my youth and the *Earthy Part of Water* in my later years. The current Magister of Coven of the Scales is a Leo and a former Fire Chief who obviously relates to *Fire*; while the Dame is a Virgo and a lawyer who associates with *the Airy Part of Earth*. As they get older and develop magically, it will be interesting to see whether these 'parts' are subject to change. For the point of this exercise, however, our current chosen points of the Compass for a magical working would be as follows:

The Crone: North
The Neophyte: West   +   The Dame: East
The Magister: South

So, here we have four people Calling the Quarters of their choice and who are not necessarily manning the Compass at the station related to their actual birth sign, but of the part of their personality that often overpowers the Star Sign. And we often *do* find ourselves altering perspective as we go through life-changing situations during our time on this earth whereas our birth sign remains the same until death.

And when a magical practitioner makes the sign of the equal-armed cross +[1] at each cardinal point of the Compass, they are evoking the protection of the Elements – not using it in any Christian context. The equal-armed cross, also referred to as the square cross is another name for the Greek cross when this is found in ancient cultures *pre-dating* Christianity.

First orient yourself by facing the North – the Place of Power – and remember that the + is shorthand for Earth (forehead), Fire (chest), Air (right shoulder) and Water (left shoulder) and by introducing it into our Circle workings we are bringing down *every* attribute, association and correspondence relating to those four points of the Compass simply by evoking the Guardian and making the sign of that cross. Even if we begin traditionally casting the Compass at the East we still follow the sequence of the equal-armed cross at each station. For example:

East + South + West + North + and complete the Circle by returning to face the East.

Hopefully a picture is beginning to emerge concerning the exactitude necessary for a serious magical undertaking whether it be for spell-casting, banishing, divination or meditation. The famous magician's directive 'Know Thyself!' is not just referring to *spiritual* self-analysis, it also exhorts us to understand exactly where we are placed in the magical and universal scheme of things.

Endnotes

1. For the purpose of examples in the text, I have used Aleister Crowley's Tarot and *The Book of Thoth* for imagery and his *Liber777* for correspondences since these are the sources with which I am most familiar on a magical level. Needless to say, many of these images will not be the same for those using other Tarot decks or Tables of Correspondences (i.e. David Conway's *The Complete Magical Primer*), but the principles remain the same.

Chapter One

Elemental Earth

When we really think about the **Earth** there are multiple images that can spring to mind. The most popular, however, is probably the world of David Attenborough where there are fabulous landscapes, wonderful wildlife and fascinating glimpses into secret places we never previously knew existed. It is a world that fills us with awe, where even the presenter speaks in such tones of hushed reverence that it's almost as though we were entering some sacred, holy place. From the comfort of our home we can scale the highest mountain peaks, trek across miles of wind-blown desert, or descend into the lush gloom of forest and jungle. When we watch the DVDs of *Planet Earth* we are participating in a monument path-working created for our delectation by the BBC!

Mountains form the most spectacular creations on the planet and cover such a large amount of Earth's landmass that they can clearly be identified from outer space. Mountains are also a perfect reminder that humans count for nothing in the greater scheme of things. They were formed by tectonic plate upheavals of such magnitude that the fossilised remains of prehistoric sea creatures can be found on the top of them; in fact, many Himalayan rocks were originally sediments on the primordial Tethys Ocean floor. And more recently, in 1980, a violent eruption tore apart the snow-capped peak of Mount St Helens in the USA, demonstrating the hugely powerful, and often devastating, internal workings of the Earth.

Nevertheless, these spectacular rocky elevations have an enduring fascination and until relatively recently in man's evolution, people saw mountains and volcanoes as the homes of wrathful gods, who vent their anger without warning, shaking the ground, and spewing fire, rocks and ash into the air. Today, science tells us otherwise but our fascination with them continues, and they remain impressive and constant reminders of the spectacular power of Earth's continuing evolution. (Luhr, *Earth*)

And from all this movement comes the riches of the planet that we take for granted. The core wealth of the planet is bored, mined, dug or blasted from the rocks to fuel an increasingly demanding global lifestyle; while a minimal amount of surface space is employed in sustaining the human race in its struggle to retain its tenuous grasp on the Earth. Let's make no bones about it, that grasp *is* tenuous since mankind is systematically destroying the one thing that has kept the planet safe for millennia – the forests.

Different types of forest are found in different regions of the world, from the dark boreal forest (*taiga*) which extends to the edge of the Arctic tundra, to the lush mixed broadleaf forests of temperate North America, Europe and Asia and the dense rainforests of the humid tropics. Forests also play a vital role in the global water and carbon cycles: in improving air quality, and in preventing soil erosion.

Of all the forests in the world, however, the one that we are the least familiar with is the gigantic boreal forest that is found in a nearly continuous belt across North America and Eurasia. Nearer to home we have a remnant in what is known as the Caledonian Forest, which takes its name from the Romans who called Scotland 'Caledonia' meaning wooded heights and which covered much of the Highlands and what we know as the Cairngorms National Park today. Those Scots Pine are directly descended from the first pines, that arrived in Scotland following the Late Glacial period around 7000 BCE and formed the westernmost outpost of the boreal forest in Europe.

Spreading over continents this vast acreage covers most of

inland Canada and Alaska, most of Sweden, Finland and inland Norway, much of Russia, and the northern parts of Kazakhstan, Mongolia and Japan. Representing 29% of the world's forest cover, the boreal forest – named after Boreas, the Greek god of the North wind – plays a significant role in the planet's biodiversity and even its climate. And not only is the Forest a living, breathing thing, it is also home to countless beliefs, customs and superstitions of the native peoples that have inhabited this inhospitable climate for thousands of years. And the North was known as the Place of Power from ancient times.

But that's just my personal take on Elemental Earth …

Earth Signs

The element of Earth is attached to the signs **Taurus, Virgo** and **Capricorn**, and all the earthy metaphors are appropriate here. Those graced by an Earth sign in their horoscope are practical, grounded and dependable. Apparently, these folks don't take big risks; rather, they much prefer a sure thing. But when we look behind the astrological symbolism of these Earth Signs, however, it paints a very different picture when we examine the magical correspondences associated with each Sign. For example:

The Bull is one of the most powerful symbols on the planet and if we turn to Michael Rice's *Power of the Bull*, we find a primal archetype of force and movement, symbolising power in nature and a religious significance that can be traced to the earliest times. Rice's examination of the evidence from earliest prehistory onwards reveals the bull to be a symbol of thrusting energy, political authority, sexual potency, economic wealth and vast subterranean powers.

Bulls are impressive creatures as a trip to any County Show will reveal but even these can't compare with the ancestor of the modern bull – the aurochs. This bull was an immense beast standing two metres to the shoulder and weighing upwards of one tonne of powerfully developed and co-ordinated flesh, muscle and bone. A formidable opponent in the chase, the aurochs must have been the cause of the loss of life of more hunters than any other of their customary prey. It was also the ultimate sacrificial animal.

According to Rice, the Epoch of the Bull (c. 4000–2000 BCE) was a period of extraordinary unity of ideas and of the means of carrying them into effect, over a very extensive part of the ancient world. For thousands of years the bull, either literally represented or abstracted in symbolic form, dominated the art of the Near East. While primitive cave art reveals some remarkable images of bulls in the numerous paintings and engravings found in European caves dating back to the Ice Age (Upper Paleolithic), roughly between 40,000 and 14,000 years ago. But it was in Egypt that the bull achieved what is perhaps its most exalted incarnation; its divinity is attested on its identification with the king and with the royal power.

Perhaps the most awesome, frightening and darkest image of the bull, however, is in that of the Minotaur, whose ancestry was both mysterious and far more complicated than his descent from an illicit Greek liaison. According to Rice, 'his forbears were the myriad of hybrid creatures which haunted the imaginations of the artists who sought to express elaborate and disturbing emotions thousands of years before the mythical Theseus entered the mythical Minotaur's subterranean lair'. Added to this we must also consider the points made by Michael Rice in *The Power of the Bull* that echo Karl Kerenyi's stellar reference *The Gods of the Greeks* to the Minoan name for the Minotaur as Asterion –'ruler of the stars'.

The bull leads his followers into some very dark caverns; literally so, since the bull is a chthonic creature ... But the bull also leads on to the stars, in what is surely his most arcane epiphany. The bull is a celestial creature as much as he is terrestrial; his presence among

*the stars has for a very long time been an element in magic and
forecasting the future ...*

In other words, he was a star, luminous and bright at the
heart of the underworld that was the labyrinth; upon him was
'conferred the hope of a return to the light'. Asterion's death,
Kerenyi suggests, was not the slaying of a monster; it was a
dark sacrificial rite and this belief goes right back to the ancient
stargazers of pre-history.

The bull later became another principal sacrificial animal
in the rites associated with the cult of Mithras, which made so
deep and lasting an impression on the world of late antiquity.
Mithraism became firmly lodged in the Roman legions which,
picking up its practices in their excursions into the eastern limits
of the Empire, carried it westwards as far as the British Isles.
The creation of the world is the central episode of Mithraic
mythology. According to the myths, the sun god sent his
messenger, the raven, to Mithras and ordered him to sacrifice the
bull. Mithras executed the order reluctantly; in many reliefs he is
seen turning aside his face in sorrow but at the very moment of
the death of the bull, a great miracle happened. The white bull
was metamorphosed into the moon; the cloak of Mithras was
transformed into the vault of the sky with the shining planets
and fixed stars.

From the time of the Chaldeans, some 5000 years ago, the
zodiacal constellation of **Taurus** has been seen as a bull. The
Greeks identified the constellation as Zeus disguised as a bull,
in whose form he abducted Europa, daughter of Agenor, king of
Phoenicia. The bull took off into the sea and swam to Crete where
he made Europa his mistress. One of their three sons, Minos,
later became king of Crete and founded the Minoan civilisation.
Only the forequarters of the bull are visible in the constellation,
as it is emerging from the waves.

The Virgin, figuratively or actually, is as much a symbol of sacrifice as the 'sacrificial god or king' in ancient superstition. The maiden is 'pure' according to the lights of her time and culture but it is probably safe to assume that it generally refers to an unmarried girl *per se* as opposed to a young married woman. In magical traditions it implies innocence, or concentration on spiritual things; or a reservoir of untapped force. Objects used in ritual magic are required to be 'virgin'. In fact, if we look at the image of the Princess of Disks (see below in Magical Images) there is nothing of the 'virgin martyr' in the symbology but rather: *'She is strong and beautiful, with an expression of intense brooding, as if about to become aware of secret wonder.'*

Iphigenia, the daughter of Agamemnon and Clytemnestra was offered as a sacrifice to enable the weather-bound Greek fleet to sail for Troy. The seer Calchas declared that Artemis required the sacrifice and the girl was sent for on the pretext of her being married to Achilles. In some versions of the story, Clytemnestra wasn't a willing party to the deed and this was the reason she killed her husband on his return from the Trojan War – in revenge for her daughter's death.

Persephone, also known as Kore in Greek mythology, was carried off by Hades to be his queen in the netherworld. Her mother, Demeter's search and lamentations form the basis for the ancient Mysteries, and we could even say that Demeter also made the sacrifice when agreeing to Hades' demands that her daughter remain in the netherworld for half of the year. And this story lies at the root of the Eleusinian Mysteries that endured until Roman times.

The zodiacal constellation of **Virgo** is the only female among the Star Signs and is usually depicted holding an ear of wheat, or carrying the scales of Libra, the adjoining constellation.

Since the beginning of recorded history Virgo has been thought to represent a great array of deities – among others she has been identified with the Babylonian fertility goddess Ishtar; Astraea, the Roman goddess of justice, and Demeter, the Greek goddess of the harvest; none of whom is very 'virginal' in the accepted sense of the word. This is one of the 'mutable' signs in traditional astrology (the others being Gemini, Sagittarius and Pisces), so termed because the Sun is 'in' them at the times of the year when one season is changing into another – here at the Autumnal Equinox – when we celebrate the beneficence of the Great Mother.

The Goat is one of life's cultural strangenesses with plenty of bad press, and an indelible link to the 'dark side' – but not necessarily evil. The animal is sometimes a symbol of agility and sometimes obstinately insists on having its own way – but it is far better known for its proverbial lechery, its stench and its link with the Devil! Another devilish link can be found in both Classical and Jewish traditions; in the latter the goat is called Azazel – the scapegoat – who is formally loaded with the sins of the people and driven out into the wilderness.

This myth provides the link between Azazel and the Watchers – or the fallen angels who brought wisdom and light to the world that the jealous and wrathful Jehovah wanted to keep in blissful ignorance. Hence their expulsion from heaven and not to mention their lusting after mortal women! Azazel was the leader of the five Watchers and was associated with Mars. The Watchers were thought of as the 'sons of god' sent to Earth to watch over mankind and often appear as our personal Guardians. The most famous and evocative representation is the 'Guardians of Time' collection of hooded statues that were developed by the artist Manfred Kielnhofer, who is sure that mankind is watched and protected by these strange characters.

In *Pan: Dark Lord of the Forest and Horned God of the Witches*, it was Alan Richardson's evocative imagery that encapsulated what those Capricorns who seek out this elusive being might find.

As you read this, Pan is opening his strange eyes with those lucid, *rectangular pupils, which give him huge peripheral vision. He is* observing you very quietly. Look up from the page, look around. He is here, now. Believe what I say! Also be aware that at this same moment there is an Inner Pan within your psyche who yearns to be aware of things from this wider perspective, who aches to take you toward the dark recesses of your mind, and the wild, tangled undergrowth of your unconscious. As you make your own path into the Wild Woods in search of the Great Pan, your nape hairs might prickle, you might see things at the new edges of your vision and strange realms might open up. If you have a frisson of fear – you are on the right path. Keep going. There is light and love there too, in abundance. This book is filled with pleasing seeds and roots that have been collected from obscure, musty corners of the mythological and literary forest. Just brooding upon them ensures that they will be planted and grow in your consciousness, often in startling ways ...

The zodiacal sign of **Capricornus** has been named for a goat since the time of the Chaldeans and Babylonians. Sometimes it is shown as a goat, but more commonly it is depicted as a goat with the tail of a fish. Several thousand years ago, the Sun reached the southernmost position in the sky (in its Winter Solstice) when it was in front of Capricornus. During this time it was overhead at a southerly latitude we call the Tropic of Capricorn, which still carries this name, although the Sun, as a result of precession is now in Sagittarius at the time of the Winter Solstice.

Magical Images

Court Cards, or **Royal Arcana,** in the Tarot are often the most complex and confusing cards to interpret. Why? Because there are so many different ways to interpret them when relating to both the spiritual and/or the mundane. Many decks differ from one another in the attributions of the suites (alternatively Pentacles,

Wands, Cups and Swords) and titles of the 'cast' (alternatively King, Queen, Knight and Page) although in all decks the suites correspond to each of the four elements. The following example comes from *The Book of Thoth*:

- A young woman, crowned and throned – for purposes of meditation, the magical image can be represented by the **Princess of Disks (Earth)** as the element on the brink of Transfiguration. Crowley's own *Thoth Tarot* depicts her with a ram's horn helmet, with her sceptre descending into the Earth where the point becomes a diamond; her shield denotes the twin spiral forces of Creation in perfect equilibrium. *'She is strong and beautiful, with an expression of intense brooding, as if about to become aware of secret wonder.'*

- Or focus on the **Prince of Disks (the Airy part of Earth)** who is the element of Earth becoming intelligible with his chariot drawn by an ox, the sacred symbol to the Element Earth. A beautiful, naked man and very strong – he holds in his hand the sceptre to symbolise the bringing forth of that which is sustenance of the Spirit into the physical plane from above.

- For meditation purposes, concentrate on the **Queen of Disks (the Watery part of Earth)**, represented by a mature woman since she is the embodiment of the dogma that the Great Work is fertility and represents the ambition of matter to take part in the great work of Creation.

- Try meditating on the **Knight of Disks (the Fiery part of Earth)**. A bearded male figure who represents gravitation and the activity of Earth as a producer of Life. He is clothed as a warrior and his helmet is crested with a stag.

Needless to say, these images will convey completely different concepts and feelings regardless of the design, and it is important that we select a Tarot deck that speaks to us on a personal level, not because it is 'pretty' or the most popular.

Magical Correspondences

There are many magical correspondences that are associated with **Elemental Earth** and although we might find lists of these in various esoteric books, I think we should heed the advice of Aleister Crowley who, while compiling his own *Liber 777*, was quick to tell the reader that those correspondences that make up their own lists would not necessarily be the same as his ... or mine ... or yours.

Names of Power

Traditional gods and goddesses from different cultures are associated with the **Element of Earth.** Earth and grain deities in Western culture were usually female; however, other Traditions focus on masculine attributes – therefore both male and female names of power can be invoked. For example:

Osiris (Egyptian),
Ceres (Roman),
Cernunnos (Celtic),
Demeter (Greek),
Gaia (Greek),
Geb (Egyptian),
Izanami (Japanese),
Khnum (Egyptian),
Pan (Greek),
Prithivi (Hindu).

Legendary Orders of Being for Earth

Gnomes – chthonic, or earth-dwelling, spirits that guard minerals and precious stones.

The Dweller on the Threshold – a metaphysical but formidable guardian.

Planetary Rulers

The Earth signs are sympathetic with Venus and Luna because of the passive receptivity of these planets.

Colour

These attributions are founded for the most part upon tradition but different cultures have different associations.

Citrine, olive, russet and black,

Black flecked yellow,

Dark brown,

Amber.

Gemstone

These attributions are founded for the most part upon tradition but different cultures have different associations (*Magic Crystals, Sacred Stones*).

Rock Crystal – especially shot through with Rutile,

Labradorite – a feldspar, suggesting storm clouds and rainbows,

Salt – is the mineral traditionally sacred to Earth,

Onyx – the dullness and blackness of Earth.

Perfume

These attributions are founded for the most part upon tradition

Dittany of Crete – said to be the most powerful of all magical perfumes.

Storax – and other dull and heavy odours.

Flora

The attributions given here are traditional but can alter between different cultures.

Oak – on account of its stability,

Ivy – because of the analogy of Earth with Malkuth (Qabalah),

All Cereals – wheat, the typical cereal being the foundation of the Pentacle.

Fauna

The attributions given here are traditional with real and imaginary animals.

Bull – a universal symbol of strength and power.

Magical Weapon

The full meaning of weapons can be found in Crowley's *Magick in Theory and Practice.*

The Pentacle of Salt – the platter of bread and salt, or sometimes salt alone, symbolise the two principal substances traditionally sacred to Earth.

Magical Powers associated with Elemental Earth

Alchemy – a magical process of transformation, creation, or combination,

Geomancy – divination from the configuration of a handful of earth or random dots,

Making of Pantacles – amulets.

General attributions of Tarot

The Four Tens of the Minor Arcana corresponding with the Qabalistic sphere of Malkuth.

From these magical correspondences, we can see a complexity that goes beyond merely placing a container of Salt to mark the North in the Compass, because since ancient times, the North has always been recognised as the 'Place of Power' with its Circumpolar Stars that never set. And although Malkuth is considered to be the Sphere of the Earth, it would be a mistake to limit this concept to the thin 'skin' we refer to as Nature. From its molten core to the outermost reaches of its atmosphere, Malkuth represents the Earth-soul – the 'subtle, psychic aspect of matter' and the elemental energies of Earth, Air, Fire and Water; the idea of which many other faiths reject the concept of divinity in physical matter. This, then, is what is meant by 'the Kingdom': the end-result of all operations since every magical working begins and ends by 'earthing' in Malkuth (*The Hollow Tree*).

Let's make no bones about it. This is the level at which we take the decision to make the first irreversible step on the Path. With this decision should also come the realisation that by giving 'every drop of blood to the cup' we will be shortening this present lifespan on the Wheel of Life by direct and deliberate action. The practice of magic is the harnessing of *natural* energies, whether it be derived from the forming of new galaxies at the furthest reaches of the Universe, or through the arousal of passion. In true esoteric learning there is no place for contaminating or restricting attitudes about what is, and isn't considered 'nice'.

So, the next time you take your place in the Compass and call upon the 'Guardian of the Watchtower of the North', or whomever, take a moment to reflect upon the magnitude of meanings and undercurrents that belong to **Elemental Earth**.

Chapter Two

Elemental Air

When we try to think about **Air**, we discover that it is much more difficult to conceptualise. My first thought is Shakespeare's immortal lines for Cleopatra: *'I am fire, I am air, my other elements I give to baser life ...'* but who or what else epitomises Air's elusive elements in our imagination? Secondly, comes wind ... clouds ... storms ...

The sky, of course, presents an eternally unfolding spectacle. As Oliver E Allen, an authority on winds and storms, described it as:

> one moment puffs of cumulus cloud skitter across it; the next, a billowing thunderhead perhaps ten miles high may loom over the horizon ... Even a scientist who knows that a rainbow is a straight-forward consequence of meteorological optics can gaze at its gentle magic with a sense of wonder ... The northern nights, properly called the aurora borealis, shimmer in swirling bands over the Arctic Circle. Such displays are actually gases that glow when particles emitted by the sun strike the upper atmosphere.

While the nineteenth-century writer John Ruskin described the aerial drama as 'almost human in its passions, almost spiritual in its tenderness, almost divine in its infinity' – not to mention, moon dogs, false suns, zodiacal light and other celestial phenomena.

In the modern world we now know all about these scientific explanations but from a magical perspective, I say let's go with the ancient world's way of looking at things. Where some two millennia ago the Roman philosopher Seneca wrote of the aurora – named for the Roman goddess of dawn – 'its gaping displays, some of a flitting and light flame-colour, some of a white light, others shining, some steadily and yellow without eruptions or rays'. And even the Bible, a passage in Maccabees describes the spectre of 'horsemen charging in mid-air, clad in garments interwoven with gold'. Or the Inuit folklore that sees the phenomenon as cast by lanterns carried by spirits guiding new arrivals to their world.

The stuff of clouds, tiny water droplets or ice crystals adrift in the atmosphere, appears when air is cooled past its dew point, the temperature at which its load of water condenses. The updrafts on a sunny day produce small, transitory puffs of cumulus cloud; the vast forcing of air upward along a frontal system can cause stratus clouds to form in layers hundreds of miles long. Countless movements of the air can further sculpt these basic kinds of cloud into formations of breathtaking beauty and variety.

And since divination is a magical attribute of Air, perhaps it's a good idea to perfect the art of **Aeromancy** using the formation of clouds and other patterns in the skies and foreseeing events by wind direction. The querent intuitively interprets the configuration of the clouds to answer questions or by predicting events and as with many other prediction methods the symbols in the sky can be deciphered in many ways. These ancient arts are no longer widely practised, however, every child has at one time or other looked up to the sky and been amazed by the gliding shapes and stories the clouds can tell. Like many of the archaic prediction methods, though the actual method of divination has been lost, the omens continue.

Nearer to the Earth's surface, the wind is a great life-giver: it distributes the rains, moderates temperatures, cleanses the atmosphere and even broadcasts seeds of many of the world's plants. Asia's great monsoons bring the rain required by crops that feed nearly half of the world's population, and for centuries the Atlantic trade winds made possible the flourishing commerce between Europe and the New World. Loved or loathed, the wind is everywhere.

Wind, however, can be deadly when it hits land at a force of 12 on the Beaufort scale (equal to or exceeding 64 knots or 118 km/h) in the form of a hurricane, or any of the other terrifying synonyms used to describe storms with a violent wind – cyclone, typhoon, tornado, tropical storm, tempest, super-storm and gale. Even those glamorous sounding winds from the Mediterranean can pack a punch if we're not prepared:

- **Tramontane** is a classical name for a northern wind. The exact form of the name and precise direction varies from country to country.

- The **Gregale** can occur during times when a low-pressure area moves through the area to the south of Malta and causes a strong, cool, northeasterly wind to affect the island. It also affects other islands of the Western Mediterranean.

- The **Levant** is an easterly wind that blows in the western Mediterranean and southern France, an example of mountain-gap wind. In the western Mediterranean, particularly when the wind blows through the Strait of Gibraltar, it is called the *Viento de Levante* or the *Levanter*. It is also known as the Solano. When blowing moderately or strongly, the Levant causes heavy swells on the Mediterranean. Usually gentle and damp, the Levant frequently brings clouds and rain; when it brings good weather, it is known as the *Levant Blanc*.

- **Sirocco/Scirocco,** is a Mediterranean wind that comes from the Sahara and can reach hurricane speeds in North Africa and Southern Europe, especially during the summer season.

- **Ostro** or **Austro**, is a southerly wind in the Mediterranean, especially the Adriatic. Its name is derived from the Latin name *Auster*, which also meant a southerly wind. It is a warm and humid wind that often carries rain, but it is also sometimes identified with the Libeccio and Scirocco.

- The **Libeccio** is the westerly or south-westerly wind which predominates in northern Corsica all year round; it frequently raises high seas and may give violent westerly squalls. In summer it is most persistent, but in winter it alternates with the Tramontane (north-east or north).

- **Ponente** is the traditional cardinal point West, more specifically a wind that blows from the west. The name is derived from Latin for 'setting', meaning sunset, and appeared by that name in the traditional compass rose on the Mediterranean nautical charts since the Middle Ages. It sometimes appears as Zephyrus, the ancient Greek name, probably derived from 'zopho' (meaning dark, gloomy, a reference to the sunset rather than the quality of the wind). Romans also called it *Favonius*, probably meaning 'favourable', as the westerly wind in the Mediterranean was regarded as a mild wind that brought relief from the summer heat and some useful moisture for crops.

- The **Mistral** is a strong, cold, northwesterly wind that blows from southern France into the Gulf of Lion in the northern Mediterranean, with sustained winds sometimes reaching 185 km/h (115 mph). It is most common in the winter and spring, and strongest in the transition between the two seasons. In France, it refers to a violent, cold, north or northwest wind that accelerates when it passes through the valleys of the Rhône and the Durance Rivers to the coast of the Mediterranean around the Camargue region. It affects the northeast of the plain of Languedoc and Provence to the east of Toulon, where it is felt as a strong west wind. It has a major influence all along the Mediterranean coast of France, and often causes sudden storms in the Mediterranean between Corsica and the Balearic Islands.

Without **Air,** however, nothing could survive on the planet. Air drives the winds that draw water from the oceans in the form of vapour, which rises to be converted into clouds and rain. Connected with 'life' and 'soul' in mythology, mysticism and magic, Air is connected with Ma'at, the Egyptian goddess of truth who was born of air, and sometimes with the card called the Fool in the Tarot; while control of breathing is an important technique in yoga towards spiritual enlightenment.

Air was not only the substance of the divine spirit but also the home of spirits in the plural. Angels, demons, ghosts and sylphs inhabited the air. The term 'sylph' was used for the winged air spirits which belonged to air as one of the four elements, the basic materials of which everything in the world was thought to be made. Breath or air as the creative spirit is also linked with the mind, the creator of ideas, and in Hinduism, the mind and breath (*prana*) are considered to be identical.

But this is just my personal take on Elemental Air ...

Air Signs

The element of Air is attached to the signs **Gemini, Libra** and **Aquarius.** It is rarefied air which usually surrounds those graced by this Element, as this is the marker of the intellectual. But when we look behind the astrological symbolism of these Air Signs, however, it paints a very different picture when we examine the magical correspondences associated with each Sign.

For example:

The Twins The mythology behind twin-brothers (twin-sisters don't appear to enter the equation!) begins with Castor and Polydeues (Pollux) – the 'heavenly twins' who hatched from an egg from their mother Leda, following her seduction by Zeus in the guise of a swan. The twins were among the heroes who sailed with Jason in the quest for the Golden Fleece and helped save the *Argo* from sinking during a storm, so the constellation of Gemini was much valued by sailors. The following lines by Macauley refer to the ball of fire (a natural electrical phenomenon known as St Elmo's Fire) which was often seen playing around the ships' masts in a storm, and which was identified with the visible presence of Castor and Pollux:

Safe comes the ship to harbour
Through billows and through gales,
If once the Great Twin Brethren
Sit shining on her sails

There is a similar combination of mythological motifs in the story of Romulus and Remus and the founding of Rome, although this ends in fratricide after a quarrel. Twin sons of Mars and a Vestal, they were first abandoned in the Tiber and rescued by a she-wolf who reared them in the Lupercal, a grotto at the foot of the Palatine Hill. Coming from such a dysfunctional parentage it is not surprising that it all ended in tears.

Twins appear in the mythologies of many cultures around the world. And as the entry in *Man, Myth & Magic* says: 'If we follow the phenomenon back into the labyrinths of religion, mythology and folklore, however, we find other aspects besides the innocent curiosity of the envious bystander. Here is also the aspect of fear ...'

Because in some myths twins are seen as ominous and in others they are seen as auspicious. Twins in mythology are often cast as two halves of the same whole, sharing a bond deeper than that of ordinary siblings, or otherwise shown as fierce rivals. Twins can represent some 'other' aspect of the Self, a *doppelgänger* or a shadow. Often one is the 'evil twin', or one may be human and one semi-divine. The twin may be a brother, or a soul-mate, such as the 'civilized' Gilgamesh and the 'wild' Enkidu.

This duality of **Gemini** can also be seen to represent the mirror image of humanity from both its dark and light sides: passive/active, positive/negative, love/hate, etc., and acts as a reminder that for every action there is a reaction. Twins can also represent the dualistic nature of the universe. In Greek mythology, Apollo and Artemis are twins, and Apollo was adopted as the sun god with Artemis as the moon goddess – but with completely different characters.

The Scales of the constellation Libra was associated with Themis, the Greek goddess of justice whose attribute was a pair of scales; and as such has come down through history as representing the guardian of justice. This aspect of Lady Justice is an allegorical personification of the moral force in judicial systems with her attributes becoming a blindfold, a balance, and a sword. The imagery originates from the personification of Justice in ancient Roman art known as Iustitia or Justitia after Latin: *Iustitia*, who was equivalent to the Greek goddess Themis. Iustitia was not a very old deity in the Roman pantheon: she was introduced by the Emperor Augustus, and though formally called a goddess, who was even given her own temple and cult shrine in Rome, it appears that she was from the beginning viewed more as an artistic symbolic personification rather than as an actual deity with religious significance.

Since the sixteenth century, Lady Justice has often been depicted wearing a blindfold to represent impartiality: the ideal that justice should be applied without regard to wealth, power, or other status. The earliest Roman coins depicted Justitia with the sword in one hand and the scale in the other, but with her eyes uncovered. Justitia was only commonly represented as 'blind' from around the end of the fifteenth century. A statue of Lady Justice stands on top of the dome of the Old Bailey courthouse in London without a blindfold; the courthouse brochures explain that this is because Lady Justice was originally not blindfolded, and because her 'maidenly form' is supposed to guarantee her impartiality which renders the blindfold redundant. Another variation is to depict a blindfolded Lady Justice as a human scale, weighing competing claims in each hand.

For the ancient Egyptians, in the portrayal of the final judgement – a popular vignette in copies of the *Book of the Dead* – the heart of the deceased is shown being weighed on the scales against the feather of Ma'at (the symbol of universal truth and harmony), the god Anubis is sometimes to be seen adjusting the balance slightly in favour of the deceased to ensure a safe entry into the underworld! All magical applications are governed by this power/energy acting as a catalyst in tipping the scales of balance that is necessary to produce a result.

During a recent magical discussion with the Dame of Coven of the Scales, she came up with a great analogy concerning magical equilibrium in that she likened it to archery. In one hand we have the longbow and in the other an arrow, but without the power of the archer's hands the arrow cannot reach its target. The archer's power/energy is the catalyst that propels the arrow and turns it into a deadly weapon – it is the archer's hand that tips the balance. If the scales of **Libra** remain in perfect balance, metaphorically there is a hung jury that cannot agree upon a verdict after extended deliberation and is unable to reach the required unanimity or supermajority.

The Water Carrier dates back as far as Babylonian times and is appropriately placed in the sky not far from a dolphin, a river, a sea serpent and a fish. Of its many mythological associations, the constellation was at times identified with Zeus pouring the waters of life down from the heavens; or Ganymede, the beautiful youth who was borne away to Olympus to become the cupbearer to the gods. From the name we would probably expect this to be a Water Sign but it belongs to Air – governing the areas of thought, philosophy and the intellect.

Perhaps the most fascinating interpretation, however, is that of Aleister Crowley's 'The Star' in the *Thoth Tarot*, which corresponds to the sign of Aquarius. Here, the image represents the Egyptian goddess Nuit, the 'Lady of the Starry Heavens'. Nuit is rarely shown in colours other than black or dark indigo, because she represents *'Before the veil of Light was created'* ... in other words, she is the 'dark womb', the 'dark matter' of the cosmos. She is shown bearing two cups, one golden cup held high above her head from which she pours the ethereal water upon it; from the silver cup she pours the immortal liquor of her life into the Great Qabalistic Sea of Binah – the sphere of 'Understanding'.

The Water Carrier is dispensing the very essence of the 'waters of life' which is a popular theme in the folklore and mythology for sacred water found throughout the world; of holy or sacred water that gives spiritual refreshment or eternal life – translation of medieval Latin: *aqua vitae.* And here there is the hint that it is not merely the drinking of the water that is important, it is the quest that will lead us to the mystical source.

On a more mundane level, we also need to take into account the long-promised 'Age of Aquarius' ... or more importantly when does it begin? And what *is* the Age of Aquarius?

As Bruce McClure, lead writer for EarthSky's popular *Tonight* pages explains:

The Age of Aquarius is not part of astronomy. It's an astrological age, which occurs because of a real motion of Earth known as the precession of the equinoxes, which, for example, causes the identity of the pole star to change over time. The cycle of precession lasts 25,800 years, and there are

12 constellations of the Zodiac. So, roughly every 2,150 years, the sun's position at the time of the March, or vernal, equinox moves in front of a new Zodiac constellation. The Age of Aquarius begins when the March equinox point moves out of the constellation Pisces and into the constellation Aquarius. When will that be? There's no definitive answer. Various interpretations give different answers to this often-asked question.

But even if you equalize the size of the signs of the Zodiac, you need to consider when the Age of Pisces started to be able to know when the Age of Aquarius begins. Apparently, there's no firm consensus among astrologers as to when the Age of Pisces began, either. And thus there is no consensus as to when the Age of Aquarius begins. In *The Book of World Horoscopes,* Nicholas Campion suggests that approximated dates for entering the Age of Aquarius range from 1447 AD to 3597 AD. Campion, by the way, is director of the Sophia Centre and Course Director of the MA in Cultural Astronomy and Astrology at the University of Wales ...

The Age of **Aquarius** was associated with the hippie movement of the 1960s and '70s, and that's where it entered popular culture, along with the 1967 smash-hit musical *Hair*, with its opening song *Aquarius*, by a musical group called the 5th Dimension. In both cases, the arrival of the Aquarian age has been associated with ... well, harmony and understanding, sympathy and trust abounding ... but it still looks like a long time coming!

Magical Images
Court Cards, or **Royal Arcana,** in the Tarot are often the most complex and confusing cards to interpret. Why? Because there are so many different ways to interpret them when relating to both the spiritual and the mundane. Many decks differ from one another in the attributions of the suites (alternatively Pentacles,

Wands, Cups and Swords) and titles of the 'cast' (alternatively King, Queen, Knight and Page) although in all decks the suites correspond to each of the four elements. The following example comes from the *The Book of Thoth:*

- A king: a sacrificial god. Crowley's **Prince of Swords (Air)** epitomises the glorious sun-king whose sacrificial death and rebirth represents the intellect. The sword in the right hand symbolises creative force; the sickle in the left hand destroys what has been created.

- From the *Thoth Tarot*, try meditating on the **Princess of Swords (the Earthy part of Air)**. A beautiful, naked woman, who represents the influence of Heaven upon Earth; she is firm and aggressive, with great practical wisdom and subtlety in material things.

- By contrast, the **Knight of Swords (the Fiery part of Air)** is an ancient bearded king, usually depicted in profile represents the 'violent power of motion to an apparently manageable element … he is fierce, delicate and courageous, but altogether the prey of his idea, which comes to him as an inspiration without reflection'.

- Try meditating on the **Queen of Swords (the Watery part of Air)** from the *Thoth Tarot* who represents the elasticity of that element and its power of transmission in the form of a Queen seated on a throne of cloud.

Needless to say, these images will convey completely different concepts and feelings regardless of the design, and it is important that we select a Tarot deck that speaks to us on a personal level, not because it is 'pretty' or the most popular.

Magical Correspondences

There are many magical correspondences that are associated with **Elemental Air** and although we might find lists of these in various esoteric books, I think we should heed the advice of Aleister Crowley who, while compiling his own *Liber 777*, was quick to tell the reader that those correspondences that make up their own lists would not necessarily be the same as his ... or mine ... or yours.

Names of Power

The list of traditional gods and goddesses associated with the **Element of Air** from different cultures is endless, with a variety of associations for air, wind, and sky. For example, from ancient Greece and Egypt:

Anemoi: the gods of the four directional winds and the heralds of the four seasons,

Boreas – the north wind was the lord of winter,

Zephyros – the west was the bringer of spring,

Euros – the east was the god of autumn, and

Notos – the south of summer.

The Daemones of the violent storm-winds.

Amaunet is an ancient Egyptian Goddess of air or wind, whose name means 'She Who is Hidden', 'The Invisible One' or 'That which is Concealed'. She is one of eight primeval deities who existed before the beginning of the world.

Venti (Roman),

Borrum (Celtic),

Tsusanoo (Japanese),

Quetzalcoatl (Aztec),

Ilmarinen (Finnish).

Legendary Orders of Being for Air

Sylphs – spirits of the Air.

Planetary Rulers

The Air signs correspond particularly with Saturn and Mercury because of their connection with thought.

Colour

These attributions are founded for the most part upon tradition but different cultures have different associations.

Bright pale yellow,
Emerald flecked with gold,
Sky blue,
Blue emerald green.

Gemstone

These attributions are founded for the most part upon tradition but different cultures have different associations (*Magic Crystals, Sacred Stones*).

Topaz – is the pure transparent yellow of Air,
Chalcedony – suggests clouds by its appearance.

Perfume

These attributions are founded for the most part upon tradition.

Galbanum – an exceedingly powerful incense and has a peculiar scent which intuitively suggests danger or even evil. *'There is a hint of hidden treachery, which is nevertheless seductive. It is an aromatic gum resin, the product of certain umbelliferous Persian plant species that has a disagreeable, bitter taste, and a peculiar, somewhat musky odour with an intense green scent'* (Aleister Crowley).

Flora

The attributions given here are traditional but can alter in different cultures.

Aspen – the tree resembles Air by its trembling.

Fauna

The attributions given here are traditional with real and imaginary animals.

Eagle – the king of birds.

Magical Weapon

The full meaning of weapons can be found in Crowley's *Magick in Theory and Practice.*

The Dagger – the characteristic elemental weapon of Air,

The Fan – this symbolises the power to direct the forces of Air.

Magical Powers associated with Elemental Air

Divination – all forms.

General attributions of Tarot

The Fool – 0, the number of unlimited potential.

From these magical correspondences, we can see a complexity that goes beyond merely placing incense to mark the East in the Compass. The East is the direction of rebirth and new thought; it is the place of the rising of the Sun and fresh beginnings. The East is often considered to be the gateway to a greater understanding of mysticism and philosophy and although the general view that mysticism and the mystical experience are essentially the same in all religions, this is untrue. On the contrary, there are important differences between, and within, the Eastern and Western traditions, which is why it is considered unwise to mix and match our sources.

The Air Signs are perhaps better adapted to weighing intellect against intuition, thoughts against feelings, but this means that they might not always be able to 'seize the moment' when it comes to recognising the opening of a gateway, or portal that elevates us to the next level of 'attainment'.

So, the next time you take your place in the Compass and call upon the 'Guardian of the Watchtower of the East', or whomever, take a moment to reflect upon the magnitude of meanings and undercurrents that belong to **Elemental Air.**

Chapter Three

Elemental Fire

When we really stop to think about **Fire** there are multiple images that can spring to mind. The most popular, however, is probably the world of Professor Brian Cox where he takes us on a tour of the star-fields of outer space and reveals the inter-galactic secrets of how *we* came into being; and the epic journey of Voyager in *The Planets*. For as Marcus Chown reminds us in *The Magic Furnace*, we are all star dust made flesh. We are all creatures of the dynamic fires of the cosmos brought down to Earth by the fiery warmth of the Sun, the blistering regurgitated molten rock from a volcano, riding on the tail of a meteorite and the immense power in the sudden burst of a lightening flash.

Fire, however, is both friend and enemy to all humans, flora and fauna, especially when thinking of it in terms of the blazing forest, the volcano belching forth a sulphurous death, or the blinding heat of the desert. And yet, deep in the darkness of the ocean, the warmth from the hydrothermal vents is the breeding ground for new life and gives us a view into the emerging world as it was back when amoeba was the most advanced life-form.

According to *Man, Myth & Magic*, Fire to those of the ancient world represented the seed of life, to which all things must at some time return. As one of the four elements in which the basic matter of creation found physical expression it symbolised the ray of light, the lightning, and gold and, in its material aspects, heat and dryness. Fire is also the agent for purification and renewal. It has been used throughout history in the rites of sacrifice, since the idea that fire embodies a form of divinity is the basic theme of the world's religions; and every civilisation, great and small, has incorporated in its pantheon of deities a god of fire.

Bonfires, known in different places as bale-fire, need-fire, will-fire or neat-fire were ignited to signal the passage of the seasons, for purposes of purification and to revive by sympathetic magic the powers of the declining sun. They were lit at various points of the year: spring, the beginning of summer, midsummer, the beginning of winter and midwinter and were times for celebration. These community fires were linked to the agrarian calendar and our ancestors held certain woods to be sacred when they were cast into the flames. The bonfire is a symbol of community spirit and welcome, of belonging and sharing – even if it's only a mug of soup and potatoes baked in the embers.

From all these images of conflagration there is also the beautiful, ethereal 'natural flames' that are none the less powerful in stimulating the imagination. One is the flame which flickers over marshy places sometimes luring lost travellers to their doom, thought to be of supernatural original and known as Will o' the Wisp or Jack o' Lantern. The phenomenon is now known to be caused by decaying vegetable matter. Similarly, fungi are peculiar beings at the best of times. Once believed to be closely related to plants, they are now understood to be more closely related to animals!

One of their strangest phenomena is 'fox fire' also sometimes called 'faere fire' – the bioluminescence created by some species of fungi present in decaying wood. Bioluminescence is the production and emission of light by a living organism and occurs widely in marine vertebrates and invertebrates, as well as in some fungi, micro-organisms including some bacteria and terrestrial invertebrates such as fireflies. The bluish-green glow was first recorded in 382 BCE, by Aristotle, whose notes refer to a light that, unlike fire, was cold to the touch; the Roman thinker Pliny the Elder also mentioned a glowing wood in the olive groves. According to Wikipedia, the 'fox' in 'foxfire' may derive from the Old French word *fols*, meaning 'false', rather than from the name of the animal but I prefer the country name, especially since the association of foxes with such fires is widespread in folklore.

And last, but certainly not least, we should never lose sight of the Path of the Hearth Fire and all its attendant superstitions, which often gets abandoned in the search for more loftier cosmic wisdom. The Hearth Fire is Love in *all* its various aspects; the source of womanly power and manly energy in its most sacred but most simplistic forms, and without it no other fire can come into existence. The Greeks (Hestia) and Romans (Vesta) had their goddesses of the Hearth and every home had its family altar on with offerings were made to the *lares familiaries,* the spirits which were particularly venerated at the domestic hearth on appropriate calendar days and on occasions of family importance. This is a warning that all would-be magicians, *both male and female,* ignore at their peril. The friendly Hearth Fire is the symbol of domesticity and peace – and is the most precious of all.

But that's merely my own take on Elemental Fire ...

Fire Signs

The **Element of Fire** is associated with the signs **Aries, Leo** and **Sagittarius**, and as one would expect, those graced by Fire are fiery, indeed. They are enthusiastic and sometimes larger than life. Just like a fire that is left untended, however, Fire signs can burn out of control – so it's best to watch those dying embers. A Fire sign is also an indicator of creativity. This element manifests itself in creative and unique ways. But when we look behind the astrological symbolism of these Fire Signs, however, it paints a very different picture when we examine the magical correspondences associated with each Sign.

The Ram: The ancient Babylonians, Egyptians, Persians and Greeks all called this constellation The Ram, and in one Greek version of the story, it later provided the Golden Fleece. It was Jason and his Argonauts who stole it from under the care of a sleepless dragon. Aries is the zodiac's first constellation since the Sun at one time was entering Aries on the day of the Vernal Equinox – the moment when it crosses from the southern to the northern half of the celestial sphere. Because of the Earth's precession, the Sun is now in Pisces at the Vernal Equinox.

Like the bull, the ram was venerated by the Egyptians for its fertility and worshipped from early times. The earliest ram-gods appear to be the *Ovis longipes palaeoaegyptica* species, with its long wavy horns and heavy build in which form Khnum of Elephantine and Banebjedet of Mendes were represented. A second species, *Ovis aries plattyra aegyptiaca* appeared somewhat later around the Twelfth Dynasty, which had a lighter build, fat tail and curved horns, the form often attributed to the god Amun. Over time the three gods merged into one and Amun was commonly represented in ram form, although with the curving horns of the *platyra* species – the other having been extinct since prehistory.

The hieroglyph showing just the ram's head is translated as 'prestige or dignity' or 'respectful fear inspired by god' but the hieroglyph for a ram (*b3*) continued to show the animal with the spiralling, twisted horns. The disappearance of the original didn't cause the abandonment of the old hieroglyph and had given its likeness to many ram-headed gods in the Egyptian pantheon; they continued to affix long horizontal horns of gilt to their mummies in memory of the extinct ram-ba!

This strange ovine also helped to create the infamous Goat of Mendes – so-called by Eliphas Levi – which was created out of a confusion caused by the Greek historian Herodotus, who visited Egypt around 450 BCE. Here he noted the sacrifice of 'goats' at Mendes in contrast to the use of sheep elsewhere in Egypt, but it is obvious that he mistook the sacred ram for a goat and as such it has passed into esoteric writing.

Other myths, Greek, Etruscan and Italian, connected prosperity with a ram bearing unusual coloured fleeces and the animal has been involved in magical ceremonies in many parts of the world. The horns of the ram also have their mystical meanings. The head and the horn of the ram are symbolic of activity and creative energy, and also as the insignia of Initiation into the secret Mysteries. At the time of the temple in Jerusalem only priests were entitled to play the ram's horn, underscoring the instrument's ambiguity: Is it music, or is it something else?

The Jews use a ram's horn known in Hebrew as a *shofar* to announce their holy days and drive away evil spirits as composer Raphael Mostel explains:

Historically, the sound of *shofar*, or ram's horn, has always been treated as something in a category by itself – not quite music, but a sound endowed with mystical and magical powers. Almost every time the Jewish or Christian holy books mention a trumpet or horn, it means the *shofar*. And in seeking the roots for music itself, the Bible claims that all musicians are descended from the great-great-great-grandson of Cain, Yuval, whose name is related to 'mountain goat'. As an instrument in biblical times, the *shofar* was used to signal not only the cycles of the moon, but as an alarm for natural calamities such as floods and earthquakes, and to announce the coming of the harvest season and celebrations.

Aries is the first sign in the zodiac and has appeared as such since around 6000 BCE when the sun entered the constellation of Aries at the Winter Solstice – 'a season equally well, if not better suited than the Spring Equinox to hold the first place in the calendar', claims Emmeline Plunkett in *Calendars & Constellations of the Ancient World*. As the centuries rolled by, slowly the stars of Aries receded from the Winter Solstice and moved steadily through almost a quarter of the great ecliptic cycle. By the second century BCE the Spring Equinox was not far from the same point of the star-marked ecliptic where the Winter Solstice had been when the first calendar-makers had 'fixed' the constellations.

The Lion: Unlike most of the zodiacal constellations, **Leo**, with its sickle (or backward question mark) tracing out a great head, really can be pictured as its namesake, a lion reclining not unlike the Egyptian Sphinx. The Babylonian and other cultures of southwest Asia associated Leo with the Sun, because the Summer Solstice occurred when the Sun was in that part of the sky.

Added to that, the size, strength and magnificence of the lion caused it to be associated in ancient time with divinity and royalty. The most powerful of the lion-gods is probably the Egyptian goddess Sekhmet whose ferocity is legendary when it comes to protecting the sun-god Re. The Egyptians also had the archaic dual earth-god Aker guarding the horizons. He is most often represented as a form of double-sphinx, consisting of two lions seated back to back; because the lions faced towards both sunrise and sunset, the god was closely associated with the journey of the sun through the underworld each night.

Mithras' cult was spread throughout the Roman Empire by the soldiers of the Legions. Mithras' original identity as a god of light was gradually intensified until he appeared as the figure of Sol Invictus, the 'unconquerable Sun'. One of the symbols of his cult was the naked lion-headed figure sometimes found in Mithraic temples; it is entwined by a serpent, with the snake's head often resting on the lion's head, with the lion's mouth open. The figure is usually represented having four wings, two keys (or a single key) and a sceptre in his hand; sometimes it is standing on a globe inscribed with a diagonal cross. Although animal-headed figures are prevalent in contemporary Egyptian and Gnostic mythological representations, the *Leontocephaline* is entirely restricted to Mithraic art.

According to *Man, Myth & Magic*, however, the symbolism, mythology and folklore of the lion differs in various regions, according to the extent to which people are familiar with it.

Among those who know the beast only by hearsay or in captivity its characteristics have been exaggerated and embellished; whereas in the lore of African tribesfolk accustomed to living among lions, they may be revered or regarded as rather stupid and ridiculous animals.

The Archer: Sagittarius is generally thought to be a centaur – half man and half horse – and usually considered to be Chiron, who is also identified with the constellation Centaurus. However, Sagittarius is seen as holding a bow, which is not in character with Chiron, who was known for his wisdom and kindness, and was the instrument of his demise. In some mythologies it is claimed that Chiron created the constellation to guide Jason and the Argonauts as they sailed on the *Argo*. Sagittarius is located on the Milky Way in the direction of the centre of the galaxy.

The centaurs were unpredictable creatures and monsters in the classical sense, in that these legendary beings combined two species in one skin. They had human heads, arms and torsos, merging into the bodies of horses. They were often savage and licentious, and yet they were possessed of mysterious wisdom and virtues far surpassing those of ordinary men, including the skill of archery. There are many Greek myths and legends concerning the origins of the centaurs but one of the most important is that Chiron was the mentor of several of the Greek 'young-bloods' of antiquity: Actaeon, Jason, Castor and Polydeuces, Achilles and Hercules. All of whom served an apprenticeship with him in the wilderness. Chiron was accidentally killed by a poison arrow from the bow of Hercules, and there was no antidote to the poison. Zeus set the kindly centaur's image in the heavens as the constellation Sagittarius, the Archer.

The ancient Greeks also regarded the centaurs as fanciful celebrants who danced on the train of Dionysus the wine-god but also believed that their own forefathers had both befriended and fought against centaurs in the remote past. This story no doubt coming from the battle fought between the centaur Eurytion's band and the Lapiths. It was this quarrel that put an end to the ancient friendship between mankind and the centaurs.

A softer, more romantic image can be found in *The Pastoral Symphony* sequence in Walt Disney's 1940 version of *Fantasia*. A mythical Greco-Roman world of colourful centaurs and 'centaurettes', cupids, fauns and other figures from classical mythology portrayed to Beethoven's music. A gathering for a festival to honour Bacchus, the god of wine, is interrupted by Zeus, who creates a storm and directs Vulcan to forge lightning bolts for him to throw at the attendees.

These legends are reflected in the **Sagittarian** quest for spiritual enlightenment, and for all their travels, adventures, escapades and fascinations they seek just one thing – Chiron's elusive bridge of wisdom that links the world of the finite to the world of the infinite.

Magical Image

Court Cards, or **Royal Arcana,** in the Tarot are often the most complex and confusing cards to interpret. Why? Because there are so many different ways to interpret them when relating to both the spiritual and the mundane. Many decks differ from one another in the attributions of the suites (alternatively Pentacles, Wands, Cups and Swords) and titles of the 'cast' (alternatively King, Queen, Knight and Page) although in all decks the suites correspond to each of the four elements. The following example comes from *The Book of Thoth*:

- A dramatic figure the **Knight of Wands (Fire)** clad in black armour astride a black horse, for which Crowley could provide no description, except that it is purely the male creative force in fire or spirit.

- A mighty warrior in his/her chariot is ideally represented in the *Thoth Tarot* by the **Princess (the Earthy part of Fire)** and the **Prince (the Airy part of Fire) of Wands.** Meditate on the swiftness and strength of the Prince in all his vigour and activity but bear in mind that he is inclined to act on impulse. The Princess is the fuel of the Fire, which implies the 'irresistible chemical attraction of the combustible substance'.

- Or the **Queen of Wands (the Watery part of Fire)** whose face 'expresses the ecstasy of one whose mind is well in-drawn to the mystery borne beneath her bosom'.

Needless to say, these images will convey completely different concepts and feelings regardless of the design, and it is important that we select a Tarot deck that speaks to us on a personal level, not because it is 'pretty' or the most popular.

Magical Correspondences

There are many magical correspondences that are associated with **Elemental Fire** and although we might find lists of these in various esoteric books, I think we should heed the advice of Aleister Crowley who, while compiling his own *Liber 777*, was quick to tell the reader that those correspondences that make up their own lists would not necessarily be the same as his ... or mine ... or yours.

Names of Power

The list of traditional gods and goddesses associated with the **Element of Fire** from different cultures is endless where we find all the solar-deities, fire-gods, gods of volcanoes and lightning, etc. and war. For example:

Taranis – fire sacrifices (Celtic),
Lugh – sun-god (Celtic),
Tonatiuh – god of the sun and ruler of the heavens (Aztec),

Xiuhtecuhtli – god of fire, day and heat (Aztec),

Ra – god of the sun (Egypt),

Sekhmet – goddess of war and of the sun, plagues and creator
of the desert (Egypt),

Sopdu – god of war and the scorching heat of the summer sun
(Egypt),

Wadjet – the fire-spitting cobra (Egypt),

Helios – sun-god (Greek),

Apollo – sun-god (Greek),

Mars – god of war (Roman),

Hestia – goddess of the hearth and its fires (Greek),

Ravi (Hindu),

Amaterasu – goddess of the sun (Japanese).

Legendary Orders of Being for Fire
Salamanders – a lizard-like creature said to live in fire or to be
able to withstand its effects.

Planetary Rulers
The fiery signs of Aries, Leo and Sagittarius partake of the
nature of Sol and Jupiter, because of the active, lordly, creative,
paternal, generous, noble and similar qualities.

Colour
These attributions are founded for the most part upon tradition
but different cultures have different associations.

Vermillion flecked crimson and emerald,

Scarlet flecked gold,

Glowing orange-scarlet,

Vermillion.

Gemstone
These attributions are founded for the most part upon tradition
but different cultures have different associations [*Magic Crystals,*

Sacred Stones].

Fire Opal – suggests the appearance of fire rising from the blackness of the matter which it consumes.

(Don't be fooled by a Dragon's Breath aka Mexican Glass Opal, or Glass Fire Opal – names that the stone has picked up. Please remember that these stones are glass and not an opal! Dragon's Breath is a glass that was made to resemble a Mexican fire opal.)

Perfume

These attributions are founded for the most part upon tradition.

Olibanum – the fiery elemental incense,

All Fiery Odours such as pepper, cinnamon, etc.

Flora

The attributions given here are traditional but can alter in different cultures.

Red Poppy – given its place only on account of its colour.

Hibiscus – all scarlet flowers might equally be placed here but the attribution is not very satisfactory as the nature of flowers in themselves is not usually fiery except that their perfume is a stimulant.

Nettle – can feel like a burn.

Fauna

The attributions given here are traditional with real and imaginary animals.

Lion – the king of animals and the Kerub of Fire.

Magical Weapon

The full meaning of weapons can be found in Crowley's *Magick in Theory and Practice.*

The Wand – the characteristic elemental weapon of Air,

The Lamp – the thurible or lamp is used to consecrate the

candidate with fire.

Magical Powers associated with Elemental Fire

Evocation – the action of 'calling',

Pyromancy – divination by fire, or by forms appearing in fire.

General attributions of Tarot

Judgement – the Aeon is the symbol for the Rise of Phoenix, it stands for a time of insight, the true understanding of the circle of life, of growing and fading.

From these magical correspondences, we can see a complexity that goes beyond merely placing a candle to mark the South in the Compass. The **Element of Fire** has many associations and not all of them obvious at the start – fire and ice, for example, may be thought of as opposites but ice *can* burn! Fire is the element of passion but also conflagration; it is the raw language of love and the destructive part of lust. Fire is the element of danger and like passion it can run amok, destroying everything in its path.

No one knows when humans first acquired fire but there is some evidence that it pre-dates *Homo sapiens*. Anthropologists suggest that the oldest campfires were tended by our predecessors – *Homo erectus* – long before Prometheus stole fire from Mount Olympus and gave it to mankind. That the Olympians were pretty miffed by this petty larceny is mirrored in the punishment inflicted on the unfortunate Titan who got bolted up to a rock with a disgruntled raptor daily tearing at his liver, for his pains.

Rebecca Rupp, in *Four Elements*, suggests that humans' first encounter with fire must have seemed like a wrathful special delivery from the gods, since it almost certainly arrived in the form of a bolt of lightning. To early man, lightning was an awesome and unmistakeable sign that whoever was up there was not a being to be trifled with. And that is probably why fire-gods are often irresponsible tricksters since of all the four elements, none is so unpredictable as fire. Periodic ground fires can actually benefit the environment but there is nothing more alarming than watching a wildfire advancing along the mountain ridge against the backdrop of the night sky.

Lightning and volcanoes are fire-starters, and in the hottest parts of the world fires can burst into being through the actions of the Sun's rays focussed through bits of crystalline quartz. Rupp also suggests that the flammable hydrocarbons seeping from seams beneath the ground in the Middle East may have touched off the firestorms that destroyed Sodom and Gomorrah, and ignited Moses's mysterious burning bush!

History is littered with accounts of gigantic conflagrations that have destroyed cities – Troy, Carthage and Rome all burned, so did London – several times. Chicago's Great Fire of 1871 was so impressive it was awarded a national holiday; Coventry's Cathedral went up in flames following an air raid during WWII as did the London docks when firestorms rampaged through the buildings – followed by Dresden five years later.

Volcanic eruptions, however, are awesome demonstrations of the pent-up heat energy stored within our planet. The molten lava can pour gently out onto the Earth's surface or be blasted through the atmosphere to be spread globally by high-level winds. Pompeii and Herculaneum were buried under twenty feet of ash when Vesuvius erupted in 79 CE and Mount Etna's largest and most famous eruption in 1669 lasted 122 days.

Even more spectacular and even larger is the sunspot activity which generates storms and flares on the surface of the Sun, capable of generating enough energy to interfere with electronic equipment on Earth. Although sunspots themselves produce only minor effects on solar emissions, the magnetic activity that accompanies the sunspots can produce dramatic changes in the ultraviolet and soft x-ray emission levels. These changes over the solar cycle have important consequences for the Earth's upper atmosphere.

It's not surprising then, that the sun-god was considered to be the supreme divinity by just about every civilisation on Earth. When working with **Elemental Fire** we encounter so many different facets that we have to stop and think for a moment about the magnitude of the magical energy we are conjuring up for our project. It is pointless invoking Sekhmet to take care of a problem when the cunning, patient energy of Bastet would suffice – and the outcome will probably be more satisfactory. Using a hammer to crack a nut is not usually the best solution.

Fire has a primordial allure. There's an irresistible fascination and magical appeal in its flickering flames, as anyone knows who has sat up late beside a flaring bonfire, or whiled away a winter's evening watching the epic stories unfold in the red-hot interior of the fireplace. For all its dangers, fire also makes us feel welcome, warm and safe.

So, the next time you take your place in the Compass and call upon the 'Guardian of the Watchtower of the South', or whomever, take a moment to reflect upon the magnitude of meanings and undercurrents that belong to **Elemental Fire.**

Chapter Four

Elemental Water

When we really stop to think about **Water** there are multiple images that can spring to mind. The most instant for me is probably the world of Jeremy Wade when he takes us into that unknown world of his *River Monsters*, where he investigates some of the most mysterious, deadly and unsolved underwater attacks – lands the finned culprit, admires it and usually lets it go! There is also a tremendous respect for the beliefs and customs of the indigenous peoples, with our intrepid angler even participating in shamanic ceremonies to ward off any ill luck since many of these creatures have negative folklore attached to them. Rivers and lakes form in all but the world's hottest, coldest and driest of places. According to *Earth*:

> They hold a small but vital proportion of the Earth's surface fresh water which is disproportionly significant, because rivers shape the land. Rivers are the most powerful erosive force on Earth – across the continents, the dominant landscape is one of hill slopes and river valleys. Given time, rivers can wear down mountains and carry them to the sea. Many rivers are old in geological terms ... Some have hollowed out vast caves and run largely underground. By comparison, most lakes are very young, temporary accumulations of water that will inevitably shrink and disappear.

Moving away from the freshwater world of murky lakes and mighty inland rivers, there's also the vast panoramic underwater seascapes of the *Blue Planet* that allows us to glimpse an almost alien water world. Oceans and seas cover over two-thirds of the Earth's surface. In fact, the volume of water contained in the oceans and seas is so great that if the Earth's surface was converted to a smooth sphere without topography, it would be covered entirely by a layer of seawater about 8,200ft deep!

> The floor beneath this great body of water includes such features as the most extensive mountain range on the planet, the deepest trench, and the largest structure built by living organisms. Life first evolved in the oceans … and they are also the driving force that powers and modifies the world's climate, transporting huge quantities of solar-derived energy across the globe in the process. (*Earth*)

Water also forms a bridge between fresh water and sea water in the shape of glaciers that cover about one-tenth of the Earth's land surface and containing over seventy-five per cent of the world's fresh water. As we've seen in *Frozen Planet*, glaciers are among the most beautiful natural phenomena, and they also have had a profound effect on terrain, carving out landscapes and transporting vast amounts of rock as they advance and retreat across remote areas of the planet. Some glaciers carry pinnacles of ice, streams of water, or even lakes on their surfaces. Others have volcanoes underneath them, colonies of worms living inside them, or long flood-water channels running through their interiors.

With all this grandeur, however, it *is* still possible to draw pleasure from listening to the sound of summer rain, the lullaby of a rippling stream or fountain, or T S Elliot's 'lucid stillness' in water moving over and around the rocks in the bed of a trout stream. Or the water sounds of a Japanese garden with *koi* gliding noiselessly beneath the surface of a pool. And then there's the more contrived and evocative orchestral water sounds of Britten's 'Four Sea Interludes' from *Peter Grimes*; Smetna's tone poem, *Vltava* (River Moldau); and Takemitsu's *I hear the water dreaming*.

As a Piscean, this is just my personal take on Elemental Water ...

Water Signs

The element of Water is associated with the signs **Cancer, Scorpio** and **Pisces**, and watery descriptions are well suited to this element: fluid, flowing, wavering. These terms can easily apply to an individual's emotions – the realm where Water most powerfully exerts its influence. Water signs are intuitive and sensitive, and like water, they often run deep but when we look behind the astrological symbolism of these Water Signs, however, it paints a very different picture when we examine the magical correspondences associated with each Sign.

The Crab: In Greek mythology, Cancer was sent to distract Hercules when he was fighting with the monster Hydra. The crab was crushed by Hercules's foot but as a reward for its efforts Hera placed it among the stars. The zodiacal sign represents the crab's claws. Millennia ago, the Sun reached its Summer Solstice (its northernmost position in the sky) when it was in front of the constellation. It was then overhead at a northern latitude we would call the Tropic of Cancer. As a result of precession, the Sun's most northerly position has now moved westwards to the border of Gemini and Taurus.

In the natural world, the crab is a type of crustacean belonging to the same family as prawns, shrimp and lobsters and there are more than 6,700 known species of crab found in waters worldwide. Most species are found in the shallower ocean waters where the crabs tend to inhabit rocky pools and coral reefs, but there are a number of freshwater crabs that inhabit the waters in rivers and lakes, as well as land-crabs. These animals have a thick plated shell which protects the crab from immediate danger and two armoured claws which the crab uses to catch its prey – although neither are much use if trodden upon by someone the size of Hercules! Crabs hunt by sitting in a dark hole and catching potential prey that swims past, allowing it to feed effectively as well as helping it to stay hidden from those that would want to eat it for dinner.

The crab is sometimes seen as a symbol of the union of opposites because it is at home, both on land and in the water; in the Tarot card for the Moon a crab is often depicted crawling onto the land from a pool. In some parts of the world crabs are seen as gods; in others they are messengers of the gods, while in Chinese symbolism they signify prosperity, success and high status. The animal symbolism of the crab deals primarily with elements of water and the moon, and carries themes of protection. As an animal totem, the crab's ambulation is worthy of note: never taking a direct (forward or head-on) route, the crab makes its way on land with a sideways tap-dancing motion.

According to Japanese folklore, the heikegani crabs contain the souls of the Heike samurai warriors who were slain at the Battle of Dan-no-ura in 1185 CE, during a war over the Japanese imperial throne. The battle, immortalized in the *Heike Monogatari* (*The Tale of Heike,*) was a pivotal moment in Japan's history, which established the first shogunate and resulted in the death of a child emperor. For the Heike samurai, surrender to the enemy was never an option; those not slain in battle, committed suicide by drowning themselves along with their young emperor. The bodies became food for the heikegani crabs that lay in wait on the sea floor to eat the remains: the samurai can be seen on the shell that bears a pattern resembling a human face.

The myths and legends surrounding the crab are mostly confined to seafaring nations, and although there are around sixty-five species of crab in the waters of the British Isles, there is a distinct lack of **Cancer** to be found in native folklore.

The Scorpion: In Greek mythology, Scorpius is the scorpion that killed Orion; hence the two constellations are set at opposite sides of the sky, to avoid further trouble between them. Near the northern end of the constellation is a line of three bright stars, with red Antares (Greek for 'rival of Mars') at its centre. Some 5,000 years ago, the Persians thought of Antares as one of the Royal Stars, a guardian of heaven. Nature shows how a scorpion has a great ability to protect itself, making Scorpion's meaning one of self-preservation. In the Greek story of Orion killed by a Scorpion for his boastfulness we also see this as a creature that can mete out Divine judgments.

Unlike the crab, the scorpion has a very long and noble pedigree and became the object of cults and spells from the earliest times in Egypt. A Pre-dynastic ruler called 'Scorpion' is portrayed on the 'scorpion mace-head' discovered at Hierakonpolis. The Egyptian goddess Serket was the principal divine personification of the scorpion and was usually depicted with a scorpion perched on her head. Another, less well-known deity, the god Shed (also described as the saviour), was linked with the scorpion and considered to afford protection against its sting.

In Mesopotamia the scorpion goddess was known as Ishhara; she was the goddess of Love and mother of the seven Sebettu. She was often identified with Ishtar as a fertility goddess. One tradition assigned her to the Semitic grain god Dagan as spouse. She sometimes acted as a judge in human affairs. Although she was firm, she was also considered fair. All oaths made to her were sacred.

Chelamma is the Hindu goddess of the South Karnataka region in India. She is scorpion-goddess and is worshipped along with the tantric goddess Kolaramma (Durga) in Kolar. While in Aztec mythology, Malinalxochitl was a sorceress and goddess of snakes, scorpions and insects of the desert. As a witch goddess, Malinalxochitl was regarded as a powerful sorceress who was so skilled she could make people suffer hallucinations and fantasize about many things. African stories likewise tie the Scorpion to death and life.

A Native American story tells of a creature swimming across

a river and a scorpion asking for a ride. The creature at first refuses fearing the scorpion's lethal sting. The scorpion uses his power of persuasion explaining that they would both drown if he used his stinger. The creature agreed to the ride, and half way to their destination the scorpion stung him. When asked why, the scorpion explains, 'it is simply my nature.' In this tale, we're reminded that the world of animal symbolism cannot completely escape the natural order of things.

Some people believed that a scorpion sting had the power to heal and they honoured the animal accordingly. From a shamanic vantage point, a scorpion as a spirit guide created a change in consciousness, the sting acting like a psychedelic mind altering drug that, when used, takes the shaman to the dream time or other spirit realms. In many cultures, scorpions have come to represent unexpected death. In approaching a victim, scorpions dance nearly playfully. It does not attack with any type of malice, but simply remains true to its nature.

The human dance with death is not always so clear-cut, but we could learn much from the scorpion's ritual. Death's sting is never far away and always a possibility. It's important to note that scorpions do not sting without reason. They would prefer to retreat and only attack when they feel themselves in danger. No matter the intention, this sting is painful and often poisonous.

In the natural world, the scorpion is classed not with insects but with spiders. They are commonly thought of as desert dwellers, but they also live in Brazilian forests, British Columbia, North Carolina, and even the Himalayas. Hardy and adaptable, scorpions have been around for hundreds of millions of years, and they are nothing if not survivors. And scientists don't know why, but they are fluorescent under ultra-violet light. In fact, the evolutionary history of scorpions goes back to the Silurian era 430 million years ago. They have adapted to a wide range of environmental conditions and can now be found on all continents except Antarctica, numbering about 1,750 described species but only about 25 of these species are known to have venom capable of killing a human being.

As we know, one of the earliest occurrences of the scorpion in culture is its inclusion, as *Scorpio*, in the twelve signs of the series of constellations known as the Zodiac by Babylonian astronomers during the Chaldean period. In South Africa and South Asia, the scorpion is a significant animal culturally, appearing as a motif in art, especially in Islamic art in the Middle East; a scorpion motif is often woven into Turkish kilim flat-weave carpets, for protection from their sting. The scorpion is perceived both as an embodiment of evil and a protective force that counters evil, such as a dervish's powers to combat evil. In another context, **Scorpius** portrays human sexuality and is used in folk medicine in South Asia especially in antidotes for scorpion stings.

The Fishes: For thousands of years, this faint zodiacal constellation has been seen either as one fish or two. In Graeco-Roman mythology, Aphrodite and her son Eros were pursued by the monster Typhon. To escape him they turned themselves into fishes and swam away, having tied their tails together to make sure they would not become separated.

Fish also have a remarkably long cultural history although they enjoyed a somewhat ambiguous position in ancient Egypt: sometimes sacred, sometimes scorned; eaten by some, denied to others. Various provinces of Egypt regarded particular fish as sacred, so that a fish which was taboo in one area could be eaten in another, something which is said to have led to occasional conflict. The king, priests and the 'blessed dead', however, were not allowed to eat fish, since it was identified with the dismemberment of Osiris.

Fish play many roles in human culture, from their economic importance in the fishing industry and fish farming, to recreational fishing, folklore, mythology, religion, art and literature. In the *Dhamma* of Buddhism, fish symbolize happiness as they have complete freedom of movement in the water; often drawn in the form of carp which are regarded in the Orient as sacred on account of their elegant beauty, size and lifespan. Among the deities said to take the form of a fish are Ika-Roa of the Polynesians, Dagon in various ancient Semitic peoples, the shark-gods of Hawaii and Matsya of the Hindus.

In the natural world fish can be both extremely beautiful and scary – from elegant Japanese *koi* to the menacing presence of a magnificent Great White shark – fish *can* make their presence felt. Then there's the artist's palette of the coral seas where exquisitely coloured fish bathe in warm, clear tropical water and brilliant sunlight and gigantic stingray glide through the water like giant, prehistoric water birds. Few fish are cuter than a fully expanded, portly puffer fish – but don't be fooled – this is the second most poisonous vertebrate on the planet. Fishermen recommend the use of thick gloves to avoid poisoning and the risk of getting bitten when removing the hook. According to *National Geographic*, the poison of a puffer fish, which has no antidote, kills by paralyzing the diaphragm, causing suffocation. Nearly all puffer fish contain tetrodotoxin, a substance that makes them taste bad (and sometimes lethal) to fish and is deadly, up to 1,200 times more poisonous than cyanide. One puffer fish has enough toxin to kill 30 adult humans!

Nearer to home, we can find the aggressive pike that live in sluggish streams and shallow, weedy places in lakes, as well as in cold, clear, rocky waters. They are typical ambush predators and lie in wait for prey, holding perfectly still for long periods, and then exhibit remarkable acceleration as they strike. The pike is an extremely effective aquatic hunter but the salmon of knowledge is the creature of legend ...

According to the story, an ordinary salmon ate nine hazelnuts that fell into the Well of Wisdom from nine hazel trees that surrounded the well. By this act, the salmon gained all of the world's knowledge and the first person to eat of its flesh would in turn gain this knowledge. Fionn mac Cumhaill ate the salmon and in so doing gained all the knowledge of the world. The deep knowledge and wisdom gained from Fintan, the Salmon of Knowledge, allowed Fionn to become the leader of the Fianna, the famed heroes of Irish myth. In Welsh mythology, the story of how the poet Taliesin received his wisdom follows a similar pattern.

The astrological symbol **Pisces** is based on a constellation of the same name, but there is a second fish constellation in the night sky. Piscis Austrinus a constellation in the southern celestial hemisphere and its name is Latin for 'the southern fish', in contrast with the larger constellation Pisces, which represents a pair of fishes. Prior to the twentieth century, it was also known as Piscis Notius and was one of the 48 constellations listed by the second-century astronomer Ptolemy, and it remains one of the 88 modern constellations. In Greek mythology, this constellation is known as the Great Fish and portrayed as swallowing the water poured out by Aquarius, the water-bearer constellation. The two fish of the constellation Pisces are said to be the offspring of the Great Fish. In Egyptian mythology, this fish saved the life of the Egyptian goddess Isis, so she placed it and its descendants into the heavens as a constellation.

According to *Man, Myth & Magic*, many meanings are embodied in the fish, reflecting the various facets of its nature. Because of its affinity with the sea, from which all life originated, it was widely held to be sacred. Like the Leviathan, the fabulous fish that bore the whole weight of the world upon its back, the cosmic fish is the symbol of the physical universe.

Magical Image

Court Cards, or **Royal Arcana,** in the Tarot are often the most complex and confusing cards to interpret. Why? Because there are so many different ways to interpret them when relating to both the spiritual and the mundane. Many decks differ from one another in the attributions of the suites (alternatively Pentacles,

Wands, Cups and Swords) and titles of the 'cast' (alternatively King, Queen, Knight and Page) although in all decks the suites correspond to each of the four elements. The following example comes from *The Book of Thoth*:

- For meditation use the **Queen of Cups** (**Water**) with its power of reception and reflection. This image is of 'extreme purity and beauty with infinite subtlety; to see the Truth of her is hardly possible, for she reflects the nature of the observer in great perfection'.

- Or the **Princess of Cups** (**the Earthy part of Water**) who represents the power of the Water to give sustenance to the idea, to support life, and to form the basis of chemical combination ... 'On a superficial examination she might be thought selfish and indolent, but this is a quite false impression; silently and effortlessly she goes about her work'.

- Or the **Prince of Cups** (**the Airy part of Water**) is a possible focus for meditation as this is a card of immense power, representing on one hand 'elasticity, volatility, hydro-static equilibrium' and on the other, 'the catalytic faculty and energy of steam'.

- Or the **Knight of Cups** (**the Fiery part of Water**) who is sensitive to external influence but not very enduring.

Needless to say, these images will convey completely different concepts and feelings regardless of the design, and it is important that we select a Tarot deck that speaks to us on a personal level, not because it is 'pretty' or the most popular.

Magical Correspondences

There are many magical correspondences that are associated with **Elemental Water** and although we might find lists of these in various esoteric books, I think we should heed the advice of Aleister Crowley who, while compiling his own *Liber 777*, was quick to tell the reader that those correspondences that make up their own lists would not necessarily be the same as his ... or mine ... or yours.

Names of Power

Traditional gods and goddesses associated with the **Element of Water** from different cultures include sea, water and rain deities, not to mention springs and wells. For example:

Neptunus (Italian),
Okeanos (Greek),
Poseidon (Greek),
Lir (Celtic),
Yu-qiang (Chinese),
Jamm (Phoenician),
Makemake (Polynesian),
Nethuns (Etruscan),
Njord (Norse),
Sedna (Inuit).

Legendary Orders of Being for Water

Nymphs, Undines and Nereids.

Planetary Rulers

Water signs are sympathetic with Mars with regards to the fact that Water possesses the fiery property of breaking up and destroying solids.

The student must be careful to avoid expressing himself by inventing false antinomies. There is a great danger in arguing backwards in the Qabalah, especially in the case of attributions of this sort. Thus the explanation of the martial nature of water must not be used to argue a watery nature in Mars, whose natural sympathy is evidently Fire. (Aleister Crowley)

Colour
These attributions are founded for the most part upon tradition but different cultures have different associations.

White flecked purple, like mother of pearl,

Deep olive green,

Sea green,

Deep blue.

Gemstone
These attributions are founded for the most part upon tradition but different cultures have different associations (*Magic Crystals, Sacred Stones*).

Beryl or Aquamarine.

Perfume
These attributions are founded for the most part upon tradition.

Onycha – now difficult to obtain; its origin was connected to certain shellfish,

Myrrh – traditionally the odour of sorrow and bitterness.

Flora
The attributions given here are traditional but can alter between different cultures.

Lotus and all water plants.

Fauna
The attributions given here are traditional with real and imaginary animals.

Eagle – Snake – Scorpion – trinity is the Kerub of Water,
Dog – on account of its being sacred to the Moon.

Magical Weapon

The full meaning of weapons can be found in Crowley's *Magick in Theory and Practice.*
The Cup – the symbol of Elemental Water,
The Wine – the Blood.

Magical Powers associated with Elemental Water

The Great Work,
Talismans,
Crystal gazing.

General attributions of Tarot

The Hanged Man – the sacrificial god.

From these magical correspondences, we can see a complexity that goes beyond merely placing a container of water to mark the West in the Compass. As Rebecca Rupp points out, we celebrate water in paint, poetry, prose and music and of all the four elements water has the most versatile voice. Water is the song of the planet, as anyone knows who has ever fallen asleep to the sound of rain on the roof. In the myths of many cultures water is an element of primal mystery, and faith in consecrated water has its roots in the distant past.

In many of the Creation myths, there existed in the beginning a chaos of water from which the world or the first gods were made. And although water is often regarded as the vital principle – the rain which fertilizes the soil, the river which irrigates it – the vital principle may alternatively be air, breath or spirit that injects vitality into the formless waters of chaos and creates form. 'Water, however, is naturally linked with life because living things cannot survive without liquid,' Rupp continues: 'Rain makes the plants grow, animals are generated by sperm and fed on milk, the unborn in the womb is lapped in waters that break at its coming, chicks form in the liquid of an egg, the sap is the life of trees, and blood is the life of men and animals.'

The story of the Deluge – with its parallels in many traditions – is an example of yet another aspect of water symbolism, which stems from the fact that too much water is as harmful to life as too little, explains Richard Cavendish in *Man, Myth & Magic*. There is in water, especially in the sea, a power of violence, turbulence and destruction that threatens life and good order.

But the waters of chaos are also the waters of potential life. Many alchemists regarded their processes as a repetition in miniature, of the process of creation described in Genesis. 'Perform no operation till all be made water,' they said, meaning that the material in the vessel, or spiritually the alchemist himself, must be reduced to the state of watery primeval chaos before 'philosophical mercury', the divine spirit of life, could move over the waters to create a new material or condition.

In modern magical systems, water is linked with the waters of chaos in Genesis and with female symbols: the cup, circle, oval and diamond. Water is also linked with the moon, which 'flows' in the sense that it constantly changes shape, and which is connected with the flow of the tides and the ebbing and flowing of all rhythms of life.

Both water and the moon are connected by any modern interpreters of Symbolism and mythology with the 'depths' of the mind, the unconscious, the swirling currents of the inner self. According to Carl Jung – exponent of the collective subconsciousness – the sea or any large expanse of water appearing in dreams and fantasies is an image of the unconscious. Here again, the depths of the self are chaotic, formless, and pregnant with violence and destruction. But they are also the wellsprings of the life of the conscious mind 'If attention is directed to the unconscious,' Jung wrote, 'the unconscious will yield up its contents, and this in turn will fructify the conscious like a fountain of living water.'

In other word, water as well as having magical properties in and of itself, is also the element of revelation – still or moving, pulls mysteriously on the mind, moving us to contemplate, plumb our inner depths. Water shows us our secrets. We 'find ourselves' in water. Or as A A Milne wrote in *Winnie-the-Pooh*:

> *Sometimes if you stand on the bottom rail of a bridge and lean*
> *over to watch the river slipping slowly away beneath you,*
> *you will suddenly know everything there is to be known.*

So, the next time you take your place in the Compass and call upon the 'Guardian of the Watchtower of the West', or whomever, take a moment to reflect upon the magnitude of meanings and undercurrents that belong to **Elemental Water**.

Chapter Five

Element of Spirit

In all honesty, the **Spirit** cannot be classed as an element in any way shape or form, but for the purpose of this text its inclusion in the contemporary mantra of: *Earth, Air, Fire, Water and Spirit* should not be overlooked. Perhaps we should more accurately refer to it as the **Realm of Spirit** since it is less tangible than the rest. We are all spiritual beings to some greater or lesser degree, and our level of spirituality depends on the depth of our psychic abilities and the way we interact with them on different planes of awareness.

A large number of people consider themselves to be spiritually inclined without having any allegiance to a particular religious path or tradition, but still manage to live their lives with an elevated sense of awareness without the need for orthodoxy or proselytising. Others loudly proclaim their 'spirituality' by not eating meat, spending £££££s on mystical accoutrements, posting inane garbage on Facebook and loudly condemning anyone who doesn't march to their particular drum. There had to be more ...

The definition given for the entry in *Man, Myth & Magic* reads as follows:

Related to Latin *spirare,* 'to breathe', the animating principle in living things, contrasted with the body or matter; a being or intelligence which has no earthly body, or is separated from it, such as an angel, demon, fairy, ghost or poltergeist; sometimes equivalent to 'soul', or sometimes distinguished from it, when man is said to be made of body, soul (roughly, emotions and feelings) and spirit (mental faculties).

But none of that resonated with me either. So I threw the question at my associates in Coven of the Scales who range from newly accepted members to Elders and Initiates, to see what they could come up with.

- The Dame came back with: 'We've been having a magical discussion about the meaning of Spirit. The Magister says it's the essence that holds the entire Universe together; it's the ether where the Ancestors dwell and can be called upon. It's everything other than Earth, Air, Fire and Water – almost like dark matter. I agree with this definition and look upon it as the fifth element. He's watching motorbike racing again now he's made his pronouncement. It can be like living with the Pythia sometimes, minus the chair!'

- Coven Elder, Alex said: 'I'm trying to remember that thing about the in-between moment between a flame becoming smoke when you blow it out. Right in the middle of fire becoming air there is Spirit. Spirit is the potential of all. I used to be able to explain it so well decades ago, now I can't remember much at all as an example. But roughly, Spirit could be the fifth element that holds the potential of all the other elements, understands the other elements and is the stuff that makes changes/bending possible.'

- Comparative newcomer from the USA, George added: 'I think of spirit as the element of self yet at the same time the absence of self. It's the point where micro and macrocosm meet, where the mundane drops away and the truth of the universe is made manifest.'

- While Shona, a 'newbie' from Australia wrote: 'Spirit is the divine spark which animates each of the elements and the lives of all contained within. Spirit is the other realms, wherein dwell the hidden kingdoms and those outside of ordinary understanding.'

- Initiates Michael and Martha added: 'The Greek *aether* comes to mind as the most rarefied component of everything, the "quintessence",' and 'Basically it is in all things seen and unseen because it is bigger than just a universal cycle it is responsible for everything. It just works on different frequencies.'

Most Western magical practitioners' goal is to 'Know Thyself' and that is reflected in using Eastern meditation techniques to give an insight into our true nature – a total state of focus that incorporates a complete togetherness of body and mind. This becomes a way of being: it also is a state of mind. Zen meditation is not only concentration, but also awareness: being aware of the continuing changes in our consciousness, of all our sensations and our automatic reactions. When Zen is combined with the ancient practice of Shinto, for example, it becomes a non-religious but highly spiritual path of enlightenment that is completely at home in the modern twenty-first-century Western culture.

Having a more spiritual outlook on life is not about winning the Health Lottery or having your home featured in *Spirit & Destiny* magazine – it's more about taking time to appreciate white clouds against the bright blue of a winter sky; the whisper of falling rain; the aroma of freshly baked bread, the perfume of sweet peas fresh from the garden; or the texture and colours of a butterfly's wings – the list is endless. What's more, if we make a practice of seeking out the spiritual element in life, we tend to find it everywhere – even on really bad, 'black dog' days.

But that's just our personal take on the Element of Spirit ...

Spirit Sign

Astrology is spiritual by nature but some horoscope signs

are especially driven by a desire for greater understanding. Nevertheless, the 'rediscovered' star sign **Ophiuchus** perhaps provides that missing link between the Ancient World and the New, because genuine seekers of the Mysteries have probably long wondered why the classic, age-old symbol for wisdom and knowledge – the serpent – is missing from the zodiac.

The Snake: Ophiuchus, entwined with the constellation of Serpens, covers a large expanse of sky and is filled with several points of interest, including some of the Milky Way's richest star clouds. Greek for 'serpent bearer', Ophiuchus, is usually identified with Asclepius, the god of medicine, since in one legend he learned about the healing powers of plants from a snake. His medical skills were so great that he could raise the dead, which was a cause of concern for Hades, god of the underworld, who persuaded his brother Zeus, to strike Asclepius dead with a thunderbolt. Zeus then placed Asclepius in the sky, in recognition of his healing skills, along with Serpens, his serpent.

Ophiuchus has been used in sidereal astrology as a thirteenth sign in addition to the twelve signs of the tropical Zodiac, because the eponymous constellation Ophiuchus (Greek: 'Serpent-bearer') as defined by the 1930 International Astronomical Union's constellation boundaries is situated behind the sun from 30 November to 18 December. True sidereal astrology uses the real size and location of the constellations in the sky; in other words, the true location of the planets at the time of a person's birth.

However, NASA threw the celestial Vulpecula (fox) amongst the Columba (doves) when a blog post for kids discussed the differences between astrology and astronomy. It pointed out that the astrological calendar created by the Babylonians no longer fits with the way the stars are aligned with Earth today, and mentions that there was a thirteenth constellation (Ophiuchus) that the Babylonians chose not to include in their calendar.

Some media outlets took that to mean that NASA had changed the astrological calendar and added a new sign, completely overlooking the fact that The National Aeronautics and Space Administration does not practise or participate in astrology; its job is space exploration not rejigging the weekly horoscope!

Strangely enough, astrologists didn't seem particularly keen on adding Ophiuchus to the zodiac line-up either, because most contemporary astrologers use the Tropical Zodiac. Though this system finds its origins in the calendar of the ancient Babylonians, which roughly correlated signs with constellations, the Tropical Zodiac is now tied to seasons, not stars. So the existence of Ophiuchus as a constellation apparently doesn't affect Earth-bound astrological charts. Nevertheless, some enterprising astrologers have risen to the occasion and character-wise, Ophiuchus persons are apparently extremely curious, open to change, passionate and very jealous too. Other Ophiuchus personality traits include explosive temper, good humour, secretive, egotistical, thirst for knowledge and sexually magnetic.

This is a star sign with all its beneficent associations with Asclepius, the god of medicine, who gained his knowledge from Serpens, the snake. Since the symbol of the sacred serpent is firmly entrenched in our psyche it doesn't take any great leap of the imagination to accept the constellation of Ophiuchus as representing **Elemental Spirit**.

Magical Image

The **Serpent** is a re-occurring theme in the Tarot and Qabalah, reflecting the fact that in the ancient world the serpent, in one guise or another, was a creature of sacred veneration despite its dangerous nature; and there is probably no creature which is found more widely distributed in the mythologies of the world than the serpent. But in the older mythologies the serpent is not always an evil being. According to *Man, Myth & Magic*, it is, however, invariably one thing – 'an unswervingly, chthonic being, as Carl Jung makes clear, a being of the primordial dark, earth-bound, underworld ways'. And as such, in the religions of man, it may pre-date even the primeval cults of the Earth Mother; certainly it has some connections with those cults, but with its own fertility and phallic implications. Douglas Hill thinks that:

> At the dawn of history, or at least in its early morning, the age-old chthonic religions faced invasions by new cultures worshipping sky-gods, gods of light. As the two groups of people met and fought, so their religions came into conflict as well ... One outcome of such conflict was that prehistoric snake cults were not entirely lost but assimilated into the beliefs of the invaders. And in Norse myth Thor was constantly fighting with the world-encircling Midgard serpent ...

None of these cosmic snakes is evil – not even the Midgard, in its world-girdling aspect, thought it may be seen as malevolent in its role as offspring of Loki and adversary of Thor. Of course, no one would deny that in myth the snake has been used often enough as a handy container for evil force, the serpent of Eden being a good example. But it is clear that world mythology does not regard the serpent motif as invariably a symbol of evil.

As in most cultures, one aspect of the snake was regarded as a source of evil and danger, and for the Egyptians it was in the principal form of the god Apophis, who threatened the sun-god during his voyage through the netherworld. Alternatively, prayers and offerings were made to the serpent-goddesses Renenutet (also goddess of agriculture and harvest) and Meretseger (also the protector of the Theban necropolis) so that snake bites could be avoided or cured. There was also a snake-god called Nehebkaw usually represented with a snake's head and tail, who serves the sun-god and accompanies him in his barque as a kind of watchman at the entrance to the beyond.

The most highly regarded serpent-deity, however, is the cobra-goddess Wedjet, who was the patroness of Lower Egypt and along with the vulture-goddess Nekhbet, a symbol of the king's rule over the two lands of Egypt. The *uraeus* (cobra), traditionally poised at the forehead of the pharaoh as a potent symbol of his kingship, was given the epithet *weret hekaw*, 'great of magic', and there was a strong association between serpents and the practice of magic. Serpents were also regarded as primeval, chthonic creatures intimately linked with the process of creation; therefore the four goddesses of the Hermopolitan Ogdoad were sometimes given snake's heads, while Kematef, the cosmogonic aspect of the god Amun, took the form of a serpent.

According to the *British Museum Dictionary of Ancient Egypt*, there was also the ouroboros, the serpent whose body coiled around the universe, eventually allowing it to bite its own tail, which served as a metaphor for the relationship between being and non-being. This serpent, the earliest surviving depiction of which is on the small golden shrine of Tutankhamun, represented the powers of resurrection and renewal, and it was thought that the representation of the sun-god was re-enacted every night within its body. While the ouroboros conveyed a sense of endless spatial length encompassing the universe, another snake called the *metwi* ('double cord') served as a manifestation of the unity of time, and a depiction from the *Book of Gates* in the tomb of Seti I shows the undulating coils of a vast snake accompanied by the hieroglyphs signifying 'lifespan'.

Most cultures with their roots in the ancient world held beneficent views concerning snakes and one of the world's most remarkable serpent deities is the god Da (or Dan) of Dahomey in West Africa. He is usually seen as a cosmic snake with tail in mouth (see above) but also a rainbow and water snake with fertility associations. Da was exported with West African slaves and morphed into Damballa, one of the principal deities of *vodun* in the New World. Yet even there he retains the form of rainbow snake – the intermediary between heaven and earth.

The snake appears in magical practice as prominently as in myth; while alchemy has its fair share of encircling serpents. It also depicts the vital spirit-substance Mercury as a winged serpent, and Hermes with winged sandals and snake-encircled caduceus. So the snake-serpent retains, in magic and mysticism, its symbolic role as the chthonic being who mediates with heaven.

Magical Correspondences

There are fewer magical correspondences associated with **Elemental Spirit** and although we might find lists of these in various esoteric books, I think we should heed the advice of Aleister Crowley who, while compiling his own *Liber 777*, was quick to tell the reader that those correspondences that make up their own lists would not necessarily be the same as his ... or mine ... or yours.

Names of Power

There are a handful of traditional gods and goddesses associated with the **Element of Spirit** according to *Liber 777*. For example:

Bacchus – (Roman) as Lord of Ecstasy – Spirit,

Iacchus – (Greek) Spirit,

Asar – (Egyptian) represents Spirit as being the ideal God in the normal man.

Legendary Orders of Being for Spirit

Socratic Genius.

Gemstone

These attributions are founded for the most part upon tradition but different cultures have different associations (*Magic Crystals, Sacred Stones*).

The Black Diamond – it is composed of carbon, the basis of the living elements.

Colour

These attributions are founded for the most part upon tradition but different cultures have different associations.

White merging into grey,

White, red, yellow, blue, black,

The seven prismatic colours, the violet being outside,

Deep purple nearly black.

Flora

The attributions given here are traditional but can alter between different cultures.

Almond in flower – the seed should be taken as representing Spirit with a slight admixture of Fire; the stem as Fire, the blossom as Water, the leaf as Air, and the fruit as Earth.

Fauna

The attributions given here are traditional with real and imaginary animals.

Sphinx,

All types of snake.

Magical Weapon

The full meaning of weapons can be found in Crowley's *Magick in Theory and Practice.*

The Winged Egg – the source of all Creation.

Magical Powers associated with Elemental Spirit

Invisibility,

Transformation,

Vision of the Genius.

General attributions of Tarot

All twenty-two Trumps.

Although Ophiuchus is a real constellation with a real mythological history, it's not the thirteenth sign of the zodiac according to the astrologers – unless you want it to be – but it is the perfect concept for the **Element of Spirit**.

In the ancient world the serpent *was* the creature of spirit – of Knowledge, Wisdom and Understanding – not to mention the ruler of the chthonic realms of the primordial world; the water snake that can live in two environments; the fire snake of the *kundalini* and the Rainbow Snake that links heaven and earth. And it's at this point we repeat the observation made by Kenneth Grant in *Hecate's Fountain* and perhaps realise how important this advice has become:

> *It may be asked, why then do we not abandon the ancient symbols in favour of the formulae of nuclear physics and quantum mechanics? The answer is that the occultist understands that contact with these energies may be established more completely through symbols so ancient that they have had time to bury themselves in the vast storehouse of the racial subconsciousness. To such symbols the Forces respond swiftly and with incalculable fullness, whereas the pseudo-symbols manufactured in the laboratory possess no link with elements in the psyche to which they can appeal. The twisting and turning tunnels explored laboriously by science lead, only too often, away from the goal. The intellectual formulæ and symbols of mathematics have been evolved too recently to serve as direct conduits. For the Old Ones, such lines of communication are dead. The magician, therefore, uses the more direct paths which long ages have been mapped out in the shadowlands of the subconsciousness.*

It is pointless stripping away all the ancient magical formulae to shoe-horn ancient wisdom into a pre-prescribed contemporary system in order to make it easier to understand, when the interior workings that drive the whole have been declared redundant. The ancient symbols, sigils, formulae, analogies and metaphors remain an integral part of the spiritual journey; just as magic is an amalgam of science and art and the stepping stone to the Mysteries. As Grant explains, these symbols are so ancient that they are firmly entrenched in the collective subconsciousness and it would be a mistake to discard them purely because they are not understood – or worse still – misunderstood.

So, the next time you take your place in the Compass, take a moment to reflect upon the magnitude of meanings and undercurrents that belong to this **Element** or **Realm of Spirit.**

The End Is Our Beginning ...

Everything in the world is made from one or more of a mere ninety-two *naturally* occurring elements and from a scientific point of view none of the 'classic' four, apart from water, were even close to being true elements. Nevertheless for over two thousand years of human history, as far as anyone knew, the elements numbered just four ...

In his sixteenth-century alchemical work *Liber de Nymphis, sylphis, pygmaeis et salamandris et de caeteris spiritibus,* the great Paracelsus identified mythological beings as belonging to one of the four elements. Part of his *Philosophia Magna,* first printed in 1566 after his death, in which he wrote to *'describe the creatures that are outside the cognizance of the light of nature, how they are to be understood, what marvellous works God has created'.* He stated that there was more bliss in describing these 'divine objects' than in describing fencing, court etiquette, cavalry, and other worldly pursuits The following is his archetypal being for each of the four elements:

Gnome, being of earth,
Undine, being of water,
Sylph, being of air,
Salamander, being of fire.

Surprisingly, this concept of elementals seems to have been conceived by Paracelsus and although he did not in fact use the term 'elemental' he regarded them not so much as spirits but as beings between creatures and spirits, generally invisible to mankind. He also referred to them by purely German terms which are roughly equivalent to 'water people', 'mountain people', and so on, using all the different forms interchangeably. In *De Meteoris* he referred to the elementals collectively as *Sagani.*

He noted that undines are similar to humans in size, while sylphs are rougher, coarser, longer, and stronger. Gnomes are short, while salamanders are long, narrow, and lean. The elementals are said to be able to move through their own elements as human beings move through air. Gnomes, for example, can move through rocks, walls, and soil. Sylphs are the closest to humans in his conception because they move through air like we do, while in fire they burn, in water they drown, and in earth, they get stuck. Paracelsus states that each one stays healthy in its particular 'chaos', as he terms it, but dies in the others (*Britannica*).

In addition, Paracelsus conceived human beings to be composed of three parts, an elemental body, a sidereal spirit, and an immortal divine soul. Elementals lacked this last part, the immortal soul. However, by marriage with a human being, the elemental and its offspring could gain a soul.

In his influential *De Occulta Philosophia*, published between 1531 and 1533, several decades before the publication of Paracelsus's *Philosophia Magna*, Heinrich Cornelius Agrippa also wrote of four classes of spirit corresponding to the four elements. He did not, however, give special names for the classes: *'In like manner they distribute these into more orders, so as some are fiery, some watery, some aerial, some terrestrial.'* Agrippa did give an extensive list of various mythological beings of this type, although without clarifying which belongs to which elemental class.

According to the entry in Wikipedia, the Rosicrucians also claimed to be able to see such elemental spirits and to be admitted to their society, it was previously necessary for the eyes to be purged with the Panacea or 'Universal Medicine', a legendary alchemical substance with miraculous curative powers. Glass globes would be prepared with one of the four elements and for one month exposed to beams of sunlight; having followed these steps the initiated would see innumerable beings immediately.

In Jainism, there is a superficially similar concept in the

ekendriya jiva, one-sensed beings with bodies (*kaya*) that are composed of a single element, albeit with a five-element system (Earth, Water, Air, Fire, and Plant), but these beings are actual physical objects and phenomena such as rocks, rain, fires and so on which are endowed with souls (*jiva*). In the Paracelsian concept, elementals are conceived more as supernatural humanoid beings which are much like human beings except for lacking souls. The Chinese zodiac also consists of five elements: Earth, Water, Fire, Wood and Metal.

Even the Four Horsemen of the Apocalypse have their original roots in the Mithraic symbolism so liberally plundered by later Christianity. Here on a temporal level the Raven represents Air, the Lion represents Fire, the Cup represents Water and the Serpent represents Earth, while on a more spiritual level of the Mysteries, the Supreme God drives a chariot drawn by four steeds which turn ceaselessly around in a fixed circle (the Pole Star). The first, 'which bears on its shining coat the signs of the planets and constellations', is sturdy and agile; the second, less vigorous wears a sombre coat with only one side illuminated by the rays of the sun; the third proceeds more slowly still while the fourth turns slowly in the same spot. At a certain moment a remarkable transformation takes place and the steeds interchange natures and merge into a single form. According to Franz Cumont in *The Mysteries of Mithra*:

> The first horse is the incarnation of fire or ether, the second of air, the third water and the fourth of earth. The accidents that befall the last-mentioned horse, the earth, represent the conflagrations and inundations which have desolated, and will in the future desolate our world; and the victory of the first horse is the symbolic image of the final conflict that shall destroy the existing order of all things.

And, there is yet another primordial four-element system that is older than (or as old as) Time, that is often overlooked by the modern mystics, and which brings science back into the equation. And these fabulous four are comprised of the most ancient and authentic Earth, Air, Fire and Water of them all. Let's think Elemental on an epic scale:

Pangaea – Earth

Two hundred million years ago all of the present continents were joined in a single land mass which geologists call Pangaea ('all-earth') and which broke up some 140-million years ago; resulting in the subsequent drift of the continents to their present positions. The rifting of Pangaea had begun with the opening up of the present North Atlantic Ocean. As Africa and North America moved apart, they separated the northern and southern continents, creating mountain ranges as vast tracts of land collided when the tectonic plates of the Earth's crust converged.

Super Nova – Air

A supernova is the cataclysmic explosion of a star that may, for a short time, outshine an entire galaxy of 100 billion ordinary stars; a star goes supernova in our galaxy about once every 20 years. Supernovae are the engines of creation, according to Marcus Chown in *The Magic Furnace*, because not only do they give birth to new elements, but they scatter those elements to the currents of space along with many of the elements forged in the normal course of a star's life via cosmic winds.

Ring of Fire – Fire

The Pacific Ocean is shrinking, pressed on all sides by advancing continents that push the ocean floor back into the deep trenches that rim its shores. And above the descending tectonic plates is a fiery necklace of volcanoes, the magnificent and deadly 'Ring of Fire'. There are nearly 800 volcanoes known to have been active on earth during historic times: five hundred of these are located on the perimeter of the Pacific. New discoveries show that this encircling Ring of Fire – where there are frequent earthquakes and powerful volcanic eruptions – had a role in causing the ancient continent of Zealandia's submersion beneath the ocean waves.

Tethys Sea – Water

According to physicist Chet Raymo, on the eastern side of Pangaea, a great wedge-shaped arm of the universal ocean intruded deeply into the super-continent, with its vertex near the present Strait of Gibraltar. This now vanished body of water takes its name from Tethys, the wife of Oceanus in Greek mythology and the mother of seas. By about 140 million years ago the Tethys Sea began to narrow and connected with the Atlantic Ocean to create an around-the-world seaway, between the northern and southern continents.

All this might go a long way to explain why much of what passes for magic today, is sterile and ineffective. And how many magical practitioners just go through the motions when setting up their Compass-Circle for a ritual because ... *'Well, it's only symbolic, isn't it?'* And how many shy away from making the sign of the equal-armed cross because ... *'Well, it's Christian, isn't it?'*

As ritual magician David Conway warns in his *The Complete Magic Primer*, to go through the ritual motions with no clear idea of what they are all about is mere superstition, not magic:

> In any case, the magician should expect more from his magic than mere signs and wonders. If these are all he is after, he would be better advised to take up conjuring, which is far less trouble. The real rewards of magical study are not temporal benefits but a spiritual maturity which affords a more profound understanding of the universe in which we live.

Let us begin celebrating these new viewpoints by taking an ordinary compass to locate the four cardinal points and place on the floor the symbols of the elements that govern them. The following examples are taken from Conway's book and in the North he suggests a rock or soil from a sacred site or 'anything gathered from the spot where two paths cross is said to be particularly effective, and that should not be too difficult to manage'. And in the South 'if you are determined to do things in grand style, you can purchase a beeswax candle from any church-supplier'. For the East 'is a sprig of mistletoe, which is particularly appropriate because of its alleged druidic connection with the Sun'. Finally the West, 'a glass of consecrated water – a pinch of salt added to a glass of rainwater'.

We all have our different methods of marking the Compass – i.e. with chalk, string, sand, etc., 'Still less trouble is a circle that is visualised by the magician but has no physical existence. In the early days, however, it is far wiser and more reassuring to have something tangible around you,' adds Conway. Whatever method we use, it is sensible to be aware that the protective Circle has no precedent in the existing Graeco-Egyptian magical papyri; where the magician wears an amulet on his person for protection.

When everything is ready, and the protective Quarters called, extinguish all lights except the elemental flame for the Element we are going to be exploring on a much deeper level – starting with **Elemental Earth (North).** Set the scene if you wish by playing an episode from *Planet Earth* (or something similar), on television in the darkened room with the sound turned off – possibly 'Mountains' or 'Seasonal Forests' – and let this lead you into the world where you can expand your own horizons of how *you* see **Elemental Earth.** This is a very basic lucid dreaming exercise to encourage the mind to start thinking at a deeper (or higher) level than mere superficial observation; if it leads into a path-working proper then settle down and enjoy the trip!

Each of these programmes last about one hour but don't be tempted to let the DVD continue playing – or attempt to explore a different Element at the same session. If you don't have a suitable DVD then use a full-page colour photograph from a coffee table book and let it draw you in. Try the exercise once a week (using different imagery each time) for one month and you'll never look at **Elemental Earth** in quite the same way ever again. The same goes for the rest of the Elements …

Remember that the equal-armed cross is magical shorthand for anything and everything concerned with the Elements and whenever we make that sign of the Greek Cross we are invoking all the powers associated with Earth, Air, Fire and Water. In fact, the school-age child of one of our members and who attends a traditional school, has been taught to make the sign of the Greek Cross whenever required to in the course of 'prayers' on the grounds of 'and that's something else they nicked off us'.

The sign for **Elemental Spirit** is, of course, the five-star Pentagram – a hieroglyphic symbol that goes back to ancient Egypt. This is made by touching the forehead with the right hand, and drawing a line down to the left thigh, up to the right shoulder, across to the left shoulder, down to the right thigh and back to forehead. We can use this as a sign of blessing or protection; or to close the Compass having completed the circle; or at the opening and closing of a celebratory rite. There are numerous ways of utilising the pentagram and these can be found in *The Complete Rituals of the Golden Dawn*.

So, at the end of our journeying our perception of what the Elements mean to us magically and mystically has (hopefully) increased one hundred-fold, and that the material bits and pieces we use at the Quarters are just markers to prevent us

breaching the circle's boundaries. On an inner level the changes will be much more profound and in our mind's eye the vision is boundless. This new 'sight' encompasses everything from the sparkling prism refracted in a dew drop (Water) when it catches the rising sun (Fire) ... to the lofty snow-covered ridges of the highest mountain range (Earth) where the atmosphere (Air) is so rarified that we can hardly breath. From the vast underground caverns hollowed out by ancient torrents ... to the towering chimneys of the deep sea thermal vents, our Elemental world is pure magic. And that in turn leads us from the beauty of an early sunrise ... to the outer reaches of deep space and the nurseries of the stars ... and beyond to the the **Realm of Spirit.**

But that's just my personal take on *Working with the Elements* ...

Sources & Bibliography

Atmosphere, Oliver E Allen (Time Life)

Book of Divining the Future, Eva Shaw (Wordsworth)

Calendars and Constellations of the Ancient World, Emmeline Plunkett (Senate)

The Complete Magical Primer, David Conway (Aquarian)

The Complete Rituals of the Golden Dawn, compiled by Israel Regardie (Black Falcon)

The Crust of Our Earth, Chet Raymo (Spectrum)

Culpeper's Medicine, Graeme Tobyn (Element)

The BM Dictionary of Ancient Egypt, Ian Shaw and Paul Nicholson (BMP)

Earth, (ed.) James F Luhr, (D&K)

Food in the Ancient World, John M Wilkins and Shaun Hill (Blackwell)

Four Elements: Water, Air, Fire, Earth, Rebecca Rupp (Profile)

The Hollow Tree, Melusine Draco (ignotus)

Journeys from the Centre of the Earth, Iain Stewart (Century)

Magic Crystals, Sacred Stones, Melusine Draco (Axis Mundi)

The Magic Furnace, Marcus Chown (Jonathon Cape)

Man, Myth & Magic, compiled by Richard Cavendish (Marshal Cavendish)

The Mysteries of Mithra, Franz Cumont (Dover)

The Oxford Companion to Classical Literature, (ed.) Sir Paul Harvey (OUP)

The Power of the Bull, Michael Rice (Routledge)

Skywatching, David Levy (Collins)

Starchild I & II, Melusine Draco (ignotus)

Author Biography

Mélusine Draco is an Initiate of traditional British Old Craft and the Khemetic Mysteries. Her highly individualistic teaching methods and writing draw on historical sources supported by academic texts and current archaeological findings; endorsing Crowley's view that magic(k) is an amalgam of science and art, and that magic is the outer route to the inner Mysteries. Author of several titles currently published with John Hunt Publishing including the best-selling six-part Traditional Witchcraft series; two titles on power animals – *Aubry's Dog* and *Black Horse, White Horse; By Spellbook & Candle; By Wolfsbane & Mandrake Root; Pan: Dark Lord of the Forest and Horned God of the Witches; The Dictionary of Magic & Mystery* published by Moon Books; *Magic Crystals Sacred Stones* and *The Atum-Re Revival* published by Axis Mundi Books. Her esoteric novels in the Temple House series are available in both paperback and e-book formats – all books are available on Amazon.

www.covenofthescales.com and www.templeofkhem.com
Blog: http://wordpress/melusincedraco/blog
Melusine Draco on Facebook
Facebook:
https://www.facebook.com/Melusine-Draco-486677478165958
Facebook: http://www.facebook.com/TradBritOldCraft
Facebook: http:// www.facebook.com/TempleofKhem
Facebook: http://www.facebook.com/TempleHouseArchive
Facebook: http://www.facebook.com/IgnotusPressUK

Other Moon Books in the Pagan Portals series by
Melusine Draco
By Spell Book and Candle: Cursing, Hexing, Bottling & Binding
By Wolfsbane & Mandrake Root: The Shadow World of Plants and

Their Poisons
Divination: By Rod, Birds & Fingers
Have a Cool Yule: How-To Survive (and Enjoy) the Mid-Winter Festival
Pan: Dark Lord of the Forest and Horned God of the Witches
Aubrey's Dog: Power Animals in Traditional Witchcraft
Black Horse, White Horse: Power Animals in Traditional Witchcraft

We think you will also enjoy...

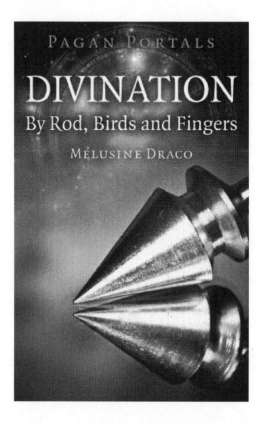

Divination: By Rod, Birds and Fingers, Melusine Draco
An Introduction to Divination

978-1-78535-858-6 (Paperback)
978-1-78535-859-3 (e-book)

Best Selling Pagan Portals & Shaman Pathways

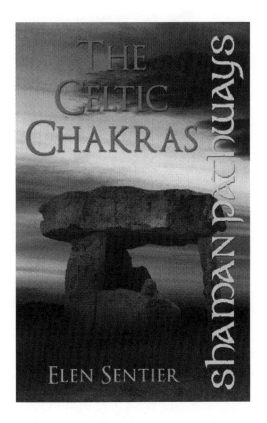

Celtic Chakras, Elen Sentier

Tread the British native shaman's path, explore the Goddess
hidden in the ancient stories; walk the Celtic chakra spiral
labyrinth.

*Rich with personal vision, the book is an interesting exploration of
wholeness*
Emma Restall Orr

978-1-78099-506-9 (paperback)
978-1-78099-507-6 (e-book)

Druid Shaman, Danu Forest

A practical guide to Celtic shamanism with exercises and techniques as well as traditional lore for exploring the Celtic Otherworld

A sound, practical introduction to a complex and wide-ranging subject
Philip Shallcrass

978-1-78099-615-8 (paperback)
978-1-78099-616-5 (e-book)

Best Selling Pagan Portals & Shaman Pathways

Kitchen Witchcraft, Rachel Patterson
Take a glimpse at the workings of a Kitchen Witch and share in
the crafts

*A wonderful little book which will get anyone started on Kitchen
Witchery. Informative, and easy to follow*
Janet Farrar & Gavin Bone

978-1-78099-843-5 (paperback)
978-1-78099-842-8 (e-book)

Best Selling Pagan Portals & Shaman Pathways

Moon Magic, Rachel Patterson

An introduction to working with the phases of the Moon

*...a delightful treasury of lore and spiritual musings that should be
essential to any planetary magic-worker's reading list.*
David Salisbury

978-1-78279-281-9 (paperback)
978-1-78279-282-6 (e-book)

Best Selling Pagan Portals & Shaman Pathways

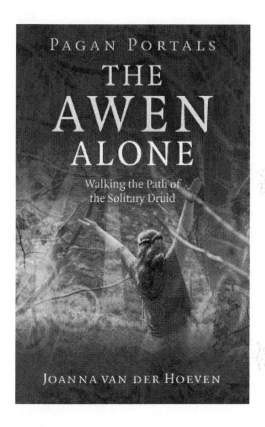

The Awen Alone, Joanna van der Hoeven
An introductory guide for the solitary Druid

Joanna's voice carries the impact and knowledge of the ancestors,
combined with the wisdom of contemporary understanding.
Cat Treadwell

978-1-78279-547-6 (paperback)
978-1-78279-546-9 (e-book)

Best Selling Pagan Portals & Shaman Pathways

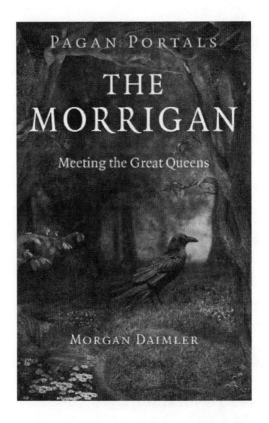

The Morrigan, Morgan Daimler

On shadowed wings and in raven's call, meet the ancient Irish
Goddess of war, battle, prophecy, death, sovereignty, and magic

*...a well-researched and heartfelt guide to the Morrigan from a fellow
devotee and priestess*
Stephanie Woodfield

978-1-78279-833-0 (paperback)
978-1-78279-834-7 (e-book)

MOON
BOOKS

PAGANISM & SHAMANISM

What is Paganism? A religion, a spirituality, an alternative
belief system, nature worship? You can find support for all these
definitions (and many more) in dictionaries, encyclopaedias, and
text books of religion, but subscribe to any one and the truth will
evade you. Above all Paganism is a creative pursuit, an encounter
with reality, an exploration of meaning and an expression of the
soul. Druids, Heathens, Wiccans and others, all contribute their
insights and literary riches to the Pagan tradition. Moon Books
invites you to begin or to deepen your own encounter, right here,
right now.
If you have enjoyed this book, why not tell other readers by
posting a review on your preferred book site. Recent bestsellers
from Moon Books are:

Journey to the Dark Goddess
How to Return to Your Soul
Jane Meredith
Discover the powerful secrets of the Dark Goddess and
transform your depression, grief and pain into healing
and integration.
Paperback: 978-1-84694-677-6 ebook: 978-1-78099-223-5

Shaman Pathways – The Druid Shaman
Exploring the Celtic Otherworld
Danu Forest
A practical guide to Celtic shamanism with exercises and
techniques as well as traditional lore for exploring the Celtic
Otherworld.
Paperback: 978-1-78099-615-8 ebook: 978-1-78099-616-5

Traditional Witchcraft for the Woods and Forests
A Witch's Guide to the Woodland with Guided Meditations and
Pathworking
Melusine Draco
A Witch's guide to walking alone in the woods, with guided
meditations and pathworking.
Paperback: 978-1-84694-803-9 ebook: 978-1-84694-804-6

Wild Earth, Wild Soul
A Manual for an Ecstatic Culture
Bill Pfeiffer
Imagine a nature-based culture so alive and so connected,
spreading like wildfire. This book is the first flame…
Paperback: 978-1-78099-187-0 ebook: 978-1-78099-188-7

Naming the Goddess
Trevor Greenfield
Naming the Goddess is written by over eighty adherents and
scholars of Goddess and Goddess Spirituality.
Paperback: 978-1-78279-476-9 ebook: 978-1-78279-475-2

Shapeshifting into Higher Consciousness
Heal and Transform Yourself and Our World with Ancient
Shamanic and Modern Methods
Llyn Roberts
Ancient and modern methods that you can use every day to
transform yourself and make a positive difference in the world.
Paperback: 978-1-84694-843-5 ebook: 978-1-84694-844-2

Readers of ebooks can buy or view any of these bestsellers by
clicking on the live link in the title. Most titles are published in
paperback and as an ebook. Paperbacks are available in traditional
bookshops. Both print and ebook formats are available online.

Find more titles and sign up to our readers' newsletter at
http://www.johnhuntpublishing.com/paganism
Follow us on Facebook at https://www.facebook.com/MoonBooks
and Twitter at https://twitter.com/MoonBooksJHP